MW01242124

Never harden your Heart

Ralph Goldsmith

Mule Dynasty

Missouri Mule Skinner Led by GPS
(God's Perspective Shown)

Ralph Goldsmith

WESTBOW
P R E S S®
A DIVISION OF THOMAS NELSON
& ZONDERVAN

Copyright © 2016 Ralph Goldsmith.

All rights reserved. No part of this book may be used or reproduced by any means, graphic, electronic, or mechanical, including photocopying, recording, taping or by any information storage retrieval system without the written permission of the author except in the case of brief quotations embodied in critical articles and reviews.

Unless otherwise noted, all Scripture quotations are from the *Holy Bible, New International Version* (NIV), copyright 1973, 1978, 1984 by Biblica, Inc. Used by permission. All rights reserved.

Scripture quotations marked (KJV) are from the King James Version of the Bible (public domain).

This book is a work of non-fiction. Unless otherwise noted, the author and the publisher make no explicit guarantees as to the accuracy of the information contained in this book and in some cases, names of people and places have been altered to protect their privacy.

WestBow Press books may be ordered through booksellers or by contacting:

WestBow Press
A Division of Thomas Nelson & Zondervan
1663 Liberty Drive
Bloomington, IN 47403
www.westbowpress.com
1 (866) 928-1240

Because of the dynamic nature of the Internet, any web addresses or links contained in this book may have changed since publication and may no longer be valid. The views expressed in this work are solely those of the author and do not necessarily reflect the views of the publisher, and the publisher hereby disclaims any responsibility for them.

Any people depicted in stock imagery provided by Thinkstock are models, and such images are being used for illustrative purposes only. Certain stock imagery © Thinkstock.

ISBN: 978-1-5127-4341-8 (sc)
ISBN: 978-1-5127-4342-5 (hc)
ISBN: 978-1-5127-4340-1 (e)

Library of Congress Control Number: 2016908207

Print information available on the last page.

WestBow Press rev. date: 5/26/2016

Acknowledgment

First, I would like to acknowledge the power of the Holy Spirit. Without the Holy Spirit there would not be a book. I am not an author. It is totally out of my character and comfort zone to do something like this. The Holy Spirit revealed the stunning truth of my life.

I had been under conviction from the Holy Spirit to put my life story in a book format. I have a disability called dyslexia. I told the Lord that writing a book would be impossible because of my disability. One day, while I was watching television, an advertisement for a computer program called Dragon Natural Speak came on. The still small voice of the Holy Spirit asked me, "What is your excuse now?" I immediately bought the program. It was the best $150 I ever spent.

Earlier I had watched a DVD series called The Truth Project. It was produced by Focus on the Family and a man named Del Tackett. It was based on a Christian worldview. The experience changed my life. This series is a treasure trove of information in verbal form. All through the series you find the nature of God in detail and His perfect plan for this world and in each and everyone's life. I would suggest that everyone buy this DVD series and experience the life-changing truth for yourself.

God gave each person a desire for self-significance. My self-esteem was incredibly low. Something was missing, but I didn't know what it was. If you search for self-significance in this world, you will come up empty. If you search for self-significance through God's power and follow that still small voice of the Holy Spirit, you will find what purpose God has for you. That is satisfying.

I would like to acknowledge my wife. She is the greatest gift that God has ever given me. She is an elementary teacher. She has stood beside me for more than forty-four years. She is truly everything that I am not. She has never criticized me or put me down for being different. Being a teacher, she has seen many children with many different kinds of disabilities. Teachers are not allowed to tell a student's parents that their child may have a disability because of the liability that the school would encounter.

Maybe if teachers could tell parents the problems their children have without putting liability on the schools, then more students would receive specialized training. However, the struggles I went through by being dyslexic made me what I am today. God uses our struggles to strengthen us in His way.

I hope this book helps you or someone you know with a disability. Life is a battlefield, from the garden of Eden on. The peace is in knowing that we have a heavenly Father who cares and is always ready to fight our battles with us. This doesn't mean that we will avoid the battle, but God will always bring us through and mold us into His image.

The Beginning

The Wake-Up Call

Why would anyone want to read a book about my life? That is the question I've been asking myself for the past two years. Although God works in the lives of everyone, I'm just a common person, known only in my small circle. I can think of a million reasons why no one would want to read my book, but this still small voice in my heart keeps telling me to write it anyway. This book could be just for my grandchildren and great-grandchildren, but maybe it's for you, too. I've learned to follow that still small voice.

I would not be where I am today if it weren't for The Truth Project. Some dear friends of mine, Denny and Elaine Lewis, invited me to view a video series produced by Focus on the Family. Elaine's brother-in-law, Del Tackett, taught the series. It got me started in examining my whole life. *Truth*—what is it? Are there absolute truths, or is truth relative, and have I been taken in by the lies of this world? Maybe these are the lies that I've told myself so many times that I believed them. You see, as Christians, we are supposed to be about truth. After going through The Truth Project, I had this overwhelming feeling that I had been deceived. I had deceived myself—but why? Who am I? I am Ralph Jones Goldsmith, but who is he?

For the first time, I truly prayed: *Lord, examine my life.* I never dreamed that God would take me up on it. Every Christian's life will be examined before the throne of God. Someday we will give an account for every word we speak. That scares me big-time.

For seven nights, when I went to bed, the Holy Spirit dealt with me all night long. He took me back to my childhood, grade school, high school, my first job, meeting my wife-to-be, my next job and how it ended, my side business, building a new home, and the elephant in the room—dyslexia.

That's right; I'm dyslexic. Dyslexia has dominated my life. People who do not have this disability will never really understand it. To help others understand it a little bit, I explain it something like this: When I see words and read them, the letters are in order and normal, but when I am looking at a plain piece of paper and trying to pull those same words and letters out of my mind, they are not in the same order. In computer language the upload is good, but the download is scrambled.

If this book is for no one else, it is dedicated to people who have dyslexia. God has a plan for every one of us, and it is a perfect plan. God transcends time, and He knows the beginning and the end, the fulfillment of His plan. I believe it depends on how well you follow the still small voice of the Holy Spirit rather than on how literate you are or are not.

I knew some of what I'm about to tell you in my own mind before those seven nights. Some of it was totally revealed to me during the seven nights. The way it affected me in my life has transformed me and my behavior today. I live now with confidence and without fear, knowing that whatever I achieve is not by my power or might but by the power of the Holy Spirit.

I grew up on a small farm near the town of Plato, Missouri, which was named after the Greek philosopher. What an incredible childhood I had. My playground was two hundred acres of farmland and two creeks, Roubidoux and Mill Creek. I am the youngest child of seven; I have two brothers and four sisters. This time of my life really could not have been better. I had brothers and sisters who loved me, doted over me, and met my every need. I was the baby of the family, and my older siblings grew up, married, and moved away. Finally the only one left at home with me was my sister Treva. I love her dearly today, but back then we argued and fussed constantly.

My father, Jones William Goldsmith, was an outdoors-type person. He loved to hunt and fish. Naturally he wanted his son to love the same things that he loved. On our farm we had a fishing hole we called the Slew. My dad brought home some wooden steps from work that he anchored to the bank of the Slew. Oh, the countless hours I spent fishing, catching frogs, and doing what all little boys do in a great place like that.

Of course, life is not complete without a faithful dog. We called ours Judy, and she was an English shepherd. Judy was not only faithful but also a protector. You see, in that area of the country, there were copperhead snakes. More than anything else,

Judy loved to kill snakes. She would kill nonpoisonous snakes instantly. With poisonous snakes such as copperheads, she was more cautious. She would attack the snakes with such ferocity that when you saw it happening, you went the other way. She would shake them and throw them and pick them up again and shake some more. We would stay back because the snake, or its parts, might hit us. Whenever I left the house, Judy was always right at my side. I know in today's society, parents wouldn't let their kids run loose the way they did then, but I truly had a Tom Sawyer and Huck Finn childhood. I spent my days playing in the creeks, fishing, catching turtles and tadpoles, and building forts in the woods.

Then along came school. In first grade I rode the school bus with my sister Treva. It was a little bit scary but exciting. My first teacher, Ms. Miller, appeared nice enough. Even so, I did not like all of her rules. Playground rules went like this: no pocketknives, no playing with rocks or sticks, no pushing and shoving. I carried a pocketknife that my father had given me to cut the strings on hay bales and of course just to whittle.

The first week of school, I saw my cousin Linda Lemmons playing jump rope with some other girls on the playground. They paused for a moment and laid the rope down. Seeing an opportunity, I grabbed the jump rope and ran to my new friend Charlie. I said, "Hey, you can be the horse, and I will be the wagon driver." I tied the rope around his waist, found a broken tree limb on the playground, and tied the other end of the rope to the broken limb. So the fun began. I yelled, "Giddyup!" Charlie started running around the playground, dragging the broken limb. Great fun!

The next thing I heard was Ms. Miller yelling out the window, "Ralph Goldsmith, get in here, now!" I had no idea that I had done anything wrong, so I left the playground and went back inside the schoolhouse. She looked at me with *this look*. She said, "I knew you were not listening to me. I told you not to play with sticks, and you stole your cousin's jump rope. You will listen to me from now on, you little Indian." She already had her ping-pong paddle sitting beside her on her desk. She turned me over her knee and gave me five or six whacks. From that moment on, I could not describe the hatred that I had for that woman. She said that I would listen from then on, but just the opposite took place. Every time I saw her, my blood boiled. I don't remember a kind word from her after that. While the other kids were getting praise, she would just look at me—and believe me, I would look back.

This was when the first signs of dyslexia showed up. In those days our reading was "See Dick run; look at Jane jump." I learned the words by looking at the pictures, but along came spelling words. I would take them home and write them over and over and over. I would go to school the next day and take the test. Sometimes I would do pretty well. When they were four- and five-letter words, I would get them right because I wrote them so many times. I actually spelled them correctly because of the hand motion. If I tried to visualize in my mind the sequences of letters, I would get them wrong every time because of the download problem in my mind. Today, when someone gives me a phone number, I cannot remember it or even write it down at that very moment. I have to break it down into two or three sections.

Memorizing my ABCs was a total impossibility because I was trying to visualize them in my mind. Ms. Miller would shake her head in amazement at me. All the other students could do them with ease. This is when I first experienced ridicule from my classmates. I felt anger and frustration, to say the least. Math wasn't as big a problem. Math was something that I could see; it was always on paper in front of me. Once I learned the concepts of adding and subtracting, I didn't do too badly. Taking something from my mind to a blank piece of paper in any correct fashion was nearly impossible.

My first year in school didn't go so well. I remember my mother picking me up from school one day. This was strange since she had never done that before. From the discussion in the pickup truck on the way home, I guessed she had had a long conversation with my teacher. It was all about my grades, and it wasn't good. I remember the disappointed look on my father's face when we got home. I heard him say, "This boy is just playing around too much. He's not being serious." My playtime was cut back big-time. I knew that something was wrong. I *was* trying, even though I hated my teacher. I wanted to be accepted by the other students. Months passed, and there was another trip home from school with my mother. Thankfully it was near the end of the school year.

One evening after school my sister Treva was rushing around trying to get ready to go to a ball game at school. Sometime during all the hustle and bustle I heard my father say, "After Treva is gone, I will help him get it done." I wondered, *What are they talking about? Maybe it is some chores that Treva and I didn't get done.* I soon wished it had been that simple.

We ate our dinner at the dinner table. You see, this table was something special. I played under it as a little boy. My mother and father had bought it during World War II, when Dad was working in Tulsa, Oklahoma, building airplanes for the war. It was beautiful; the woodwork and hand carvings on the legs fascinated me as a little boy. I actually made a replica of it many years later, and we have it in our kitchen today.

After dinner was done and Treva was gone, Mother and Dad came into the room and called me to the table. We had a blackboard on the south side of the wall right by the table. Dad was already writing the ABCs on it. He said, "Son, come here." He sat me up on the table facing the blackboard. "Son, I want you to tell me the ABCs."

"No problem, Dad." I recited them from beginning to end without a problem. The problem came when he turned me around where I could not see them. I could not get any further than three or four letters until I started mixing them up. This went on for what seemed like hours to me. Over and over this pattern went on. When I could see them, there was no problem, but I could not put them in order in my mind. He would make me write them on the blackboard below the ones that he wrote, but nothing worked.

My dad became extremely frustrated, raising his voice, until finally he became so frustrated that he slapped me across the face, grabbed me by the chin, looked me square in the eye, and said, "You are not stupid, so don't act like it." By this time, of course, I was crying profusely. He walked away. I don't remember him speaking to me for days. I remember thinking, *I must be stupid, since all the other kids can do this. Why can't I?* There was a lie seed planted by Satan to destroy my life. This had to be the most dramatic moment of my entire life. I remember it today like it was yesterday.

Not too long after I was married, my wife and I were playing around, and she slapped me—in play. It was not hard, but nevertheless it was a slap. I informed her she must never do that again. I told her if she did, I wasn't sure how I would react, because it made my blood boil. I told her a little bit about the story with my father so she would understand.

The incident over the ABCs shaped my life in many ways. I was totally convinced that I was flawed in some way and that my brothers and sisters were somehow favored over me. Then one Saturday, on our way back from town, my mother informed me that I would be taking the first grade over again. I cried. The first thing out of my mouth was "Will I have Ms. Miller again?" When she said I would have Mrs. Brown, I looked up and stopped crying. Sometimes on Sunday afternoons her son, my cousin, would come home with me after church and play on the farm. I saw Mrs. Brown every Sunday, and she was always kind and nice, so my fears subsided somewhat.

I passed first grade with Mrs. Brown. In second grade I had Mrs. Brown again and passed. I started third grade with Mrs. Cook. Now this woman was a little different. She would walk around the classroom with a ruler in her hand. If you got off task, the ruler would be used on your hand, but she treated all the kids the same. My reading was improving, but my spelling was still atrocious.

I remember bringing grade cards home and my father looking at me and shaking his head. "Are you trying?" he would ask. If he only knew how hard. I would write my spelling words over and over and over and over. If I wrote them enough times, sometimes, I could get them right the next day. Those same words a day or two later were impossible, or so it seemed.

My father's look of disgust when my grade card came in would tell the story, at least in my mind. I knew he felt that I was inferior. When family and friends would come to visit, Dad loved to tell stories about Herbert, Edwin, and my other siblings. That told me how proud he was of them, but being the baby of the family, you are the last one in line. I'm sure my father was proud of me; he just didn't know how to show it. At that age, what do you have to judge your life by other than a silly grade card? I was determined to somehow make him proud of me.

A Glimmer of Hope

In fourth grade I had Mrs. Southard. This was the first teacher who ever took a personal interest in me, that I recognized anyway. Mrs. Brown was sweet and kind, but I never felt the one-on-one connection.

One day in our fourth-grade class, Mrs. Southard had a handsaw and a board that she needed sawed in two. I saw her struggling to begin the cut in the right location on the board. I leapt from my chair and said, "Mrs. Southard, this is the way you do it."

She looked at me and saw my confidence, and instead of dismissing me, she handed me the board and saw and said, "Show me how it's done."

I grabbed the board, secured it to the edge of her desk with my knee, and explained to her. "The process goes like this. You put your thumb beside the line where you want to cut, pull the saw backwards a few times to make a notch in the wood before you push forward on it so that the saw does not jump around on you."

After I finished cutting the board in two, she looked at me with astonished eyes. Then she made the first positive statement that I can remember about my life. She said, "Young man, you have a talent. You are going to be quite a craftsman someday." Another moment I have never forgotten. With dyslexia, I cannot tell you how important positive comments are.

Nor can I possibly explain the negative comments and experiences I received, like the countless times being called to the blackboard to write something and hear the laughter behind me. Or the third-grade spelling bee when I was out on first round, hearing someone say, "There goes Ralphie." School was getting harder and harder for me each year. Taking tests was brutal, and spelling words were getting longer and harder to memorize. No one recognized that I was dyslexic and gave me special training. Determined never to fail another grade again, what was I to do? I was *not* going to fail. I wanted to make Mrs. Southard proud of me, and of course my father, so my grade cards had to get better.

My career of cheating, or maybe I should say my career of survival, began. Over time I became quite crafty at it. I even had some friends, with more compassion than some adults, who helped me with cheating, but the guilt was killing me.

My fourth-grade year was a life-changing one for me. I went to Sunday school every Sunday and church every Sunday night and many Wednesday nights. My mother was a devout Christian. She read Bible stories to us children from the thick red-bound Bible storybook. We had a TV, but reading was a big part of my father's and mother's life. Dad read Western novels; mother would read the Bible and Christian books.

One book in particular that I remember my mother reading was *Angel Unaware* by Dale Evans. I remember my mother trying to explain to my father the things that Dale was telling about in her book. She was sometimes in tears while reading it. I became quite fascinated. I listened to every word that she spoke to my father about the book. Dad seemed little interested. Finally, after being interrupted several times from his reading, Dad blurted out, "I'd rather not hear any more about that stupid child of theirs. Besides, who would want to tell the world that they had a child like that? It doesn't make sense to me."

When you're in the fourth grade you do not understand a lot of things. It wasn't until many years later that I realized the child they were referring to was not stupid but had Down syndrome. But to me it was confirmation that my father thought very little of me. I'm not saying that he didn't show me love. He took me fishing and hunting and got me a dog. He even bought a horse for me. The horse was incredible. I named him Cocoa.

However, buying you things, even showing love for you, is not the same thing as respect. Somehow even as a fourth-grader I realized that respect must be earned, and I set out on the mission of earning it. I knew that it was impossible to earn it with a grade card, so I started doing things that seemed more natural to me. I started building things. I had a hatchet. I would show my father the forts that I had built out of limbs and trees. I remember bringing home clay animals that I had made in art.

My big brother, Herbert, is, very special to me. He had moved to
California. My parents said that he was in school out there. They
said he was learning to be an engineer. That didn't mean all that
much to me, but when they told me that he was working for Jolly
Green Giant, I thought *Cool,* and that was before cool was cool. I
remember one spring when Herbert came home from California
and spent some time with me. You will never know how much
that meant to me. You see, Dad was always working, at Fort
Leonard Wood army base or on the farm. When my brother came
home and gave me tips on how to hit a baseball and played catch
with me, it was great. To top it off he went in the house one day
and came out with a .22 rifle. He held it up to my shoulder and
then produced a handsaw and cut off the stock so it would fit me.
He said, "Brother, this is yours now." He started giving me safety

tips on what to do and what not to do. He showed me how to aim it and the proper way to squeeze the trigger.

My dad found out what Herbert had done. I thought, *Oh no, this will be the end of it*, but it wasn't. He began giving me the same safety tips and gave me a list of things that I could shoot and could not shoot. The list went something like this. "Son, there are varmints in this world, and you can kill as many of those as you want." He listed some of them: coons, possums, skunks, crows, sparrows, and groundhogs. "Things not to kill are things that help us, like barn swallows and black snakes. Of course you can kill copperheads, but don't go looking for them. You can kill things to eat, but don't kill one unless you plan to eat it, like rabbits and squirrels." I asked about deer. He said, "No, this gun is too small, but someday I'll take you deer hunting." I know now my dad loved me dearly. His father died when he was only eight years old, and then his stepfather died when he was sixteen. I thought maybe he didn't understand the role of a father himself.

Believe it or not, I was pretty much given free rein with the .22 rifle. The rabbits and squirrels had to be killed during their season. I was always so proud when I brought home a squirrel or rabbit for supper. Mother was always faithful to cook it, either then or the next day. Didn't I tell you that I had a Tom Sawyer and Huckleberry Finn kind of childhood? It was great! After this I started feeling that I had gotten a little bit of respect. There's something about bringing home the bacon that makes you feel good. I would ride my horse with my .22, my dog Judy coming along, and hunting groundhogs as though they were vicious bears.

My father loved to tell stories about the horses the he used to own, about the tricks they could do and all the activities that they performed. He told about the mules that he cleared timber with when they were building Lake of the Ozarks. He told about when his stepdad passed away and he took these mules and worked WPA

(Works Progress Administration) during the Depression. He told about being hurt on the job, catching pneumonia, and almost dying. These mules were the greatest animals on earth, according to him. He worked them all day, by using voice commands. I didn't think much about those stories then, but now they have great meaning to me.

I was interested in my horse Cocoa. I wanted to be the best horseman on the earth. These were the days of Roy Rogers and Trigger. I would come home from school and run to turn on the TV, unfortunately just in time to hear the ending of "Happy Trails." The bus always took too long to get home. There were no DVRs then. With my dad's interest in horses, I knew that this was a way to earn his respect. He taught me different things about horsemanship, like the proper way to brush and saddle my horse. When he brought up the idea of joining the Roby saddle club. I thought, *This is going to be it. This will help me gain respect from my dad.*

The saddle club meetings were always on Wednesday evenings. Dad informed my mother about our great idea. From the other room I heard my mother wasn't happy. She said, "Wednesday night is church night, and you want to go to saddle club." You've got to understand my mother never spoke up to my father that way. You just didn't do that. However, this night she did speak up. Her lines went something like this: "All those people do over there is chew tobacco, smoke, cuss, and act like fools. You always said that I can take the children to church, and Wednesday night is church night."

That was all I needed to hear. This was the one thing that my dad and I were excited about together, and my mother killed it. Dad and I had already set up a pattern for barrel racing out in the pasture. We didn't have barrels, so we set up odds and ends as obstacles. The next day I remember sitting on my horse near the pattern. Brokenhearted, I prayed, "Lord, help my mother to understand that I can be a Christian cowboy." That was a prayer I prayed from a pure heart. Mother ought to have known that cowboys could be Christians. She had read Dale's book.

We did get to the saddle club a few times, but not consistently. The attention that my dad was giving me soon wore off, back to some of the same old feelings. But I didn't stop riding. I enjoyed it so much. Cocoa was a small horse, half Shetland pony and half quarter horse. We did join 4-H club and started showing my horse.

The Engineer Within

With dad working a full-time job, his time was short. He gave me a big project to do. Our cattle barn needed a good cleaning, if you know what I mean. It was a long barn with hay in the middle and feed stalls on each side. Along those sides, the manure was about seven inches thick. My father told me that if I would clean out each side of the barn that spring, he would give me one calf for each side. I said, "Great." So each evening and every Saturday for weeks I spent cleaning the barn. The two calves I received we also showed at 4-H. I was quite proud. You see, working hard, especially with my hands, seemed to come naturally. It amazes me how talented you can be in one area while handicapped in another.

I seem to have a flair for mechanical things as well. The firing pin on the .22 rifle eventually wore down and stopped working. I realized why my rifle was not firing properly, so I disassembled it, took the firing pin out, and showed it to my dad. He didn't seem all that concerned, but it was important to me. During World War II, when my father was working in the airplane factory, he told me, workers would drop bolts and nuts on the floor. The next day

21

when they came in for work, these bolts and nuts had been swept to a corner on the floor. During their breaks the employees could pick up the scraps on the floor and take them home. My dad had boxes of these. Without help I took one of these aircraft bolts and a hammer and pounded it flat, the same thickness as the firing pin in my gun. Then I started working on it with a file. After several hours and many tries, the firing pin fit my gun. What a sense of accomplishment.

Building things, designing things, seemed to flow naturally out of my spirit. We often spent time visiting my cousins, Jerry and Leroy Goldsmith. We had fun times playing hide-and-seek at night in the dark while our parents spent time inside. On one of our visits Leroy and Jerry had built a two-wheeled card for their horse. After we took rides in it that night, my mind was set. If Leroy and Jerry could do that so could I, even though they were older than I was. The next week I took wheels off an old planter, cut down some tree limbs for staves to put the horse between, and of course, a lot more of those aircraft bolts. Soon I had a cart. My mother came out and looked at it and shook her head in amazement. My father came home about that time. He said, "Son, your horse isn't trained to do that, and you'll kill yourself on that thing." He instructed me to tear it apart and put the wheels back on the planter. It was my first horse-drawn vehicle. Little did I know that it would not be my last.

School still was not going very well. Being ridiculed and looked down on by classmates was demoralizing, besides the utter fear of bringing home a grade card. About this time my father started having health problems. He had his first heart attack at the age of forty-seven. I began spending more time with my grandparents, John and Bessie Cunningham.

To explain these two people to you may be impossible. My mother always called them Papa and Mama. She loved to tell stories of when she was a little girl. Grandpa had a blacksmith shop, which was just heaven to me. He built wagon wheels, he had a forge, big hammers, little ones, and pliers. It was a dream place to play and try to build things. His barn was filled with old harnesses. It is like stepping back in time.

Grandma was incredible. As a little boy the peace and serenity in her eyes and her voice was so calming. This woman walked daily by the Holy Spirit. All my life I have heard stories about her life—how she led home church and preached in brush arbor meetings. In a mostly Baptist area she did receive some ridicule. Her prayer life was something to behold, not loud and boisterous but honest and pure. Going to church with her every Sunday was a treat. Leading the church in prayer, speaking by the Holy Spirit, she touched everyone's hearts without being condemning. My mother told how she would be playing as a little girl and not be able to find her mother. She would open the door to the attic, walk up a few steps, and hear her praying for her family, both born and unborn. We still benefit from her prayers.

Spending the night at Grandma's and Grandpa's was fun but also challenging for a little boy. Evenings were very quiet while they sat in their chairs reading their Bibles. Every night before bed we knelt and prayed. To a fourth-grade little boy it seemed like hours.

It's funny how grandparents can say something to you that for some reason goes straight to your heart. One night during Grandma's prayers, after going through a long list of people she prayed for, she came to me. To me it was more like a prophecy than a prayer. She spoke blessing on me, prayed for God's hand to guide me, for God's provisions, and then began to list them. After being half asleep on my knees, with numbness in my legs, I began to listen.

You see, after watching this dear sweet woman's life, I knew that God listened to her. I had heard in church so many times that all things are possible if you only believed. If Grandma was concerned about me, maybe God was too. Grandma prayed, "Lord, prepare a wife for my grandson." *What?! A wife? You've got to be kidding me! I'm in the fourth grade. How about helping me spell?* She went on and explained the kind of woman that she would be, namely a helpmate. "Help her to be everything that Ralph is not and loving and supportive in all that Ralph does in life." Grandma was dedicated to her children and grandchildren. "May the Holy Spirit direct their lives in every way. May Ralph be fruitful and prosper and be favored in all that he does." I may not have completely understood the prayer that night, but it might have been the first time that I felt the Holy Spirit in my own heart.

Yes, by now I had learned how to cheat in school, and with my friends' help, I was pretty good at it. I would listen in school and learn things in my mind, but putting anything on paper was still almost impossible. Cheating was like a lie, and I knew it was a sin. Guilt was gripping my heart. Could I really be favored in all that I do? Could God heal me of what I thought was stupidity? My father told me not to act stupid. To me, that meant not letting anybody know. But I knew, and maybe, just maybe, God could help me. See, Grandma's life was so at peace you could see that she was totally surrendered to God, who she loved so much. Could I have that too? Could all things be possible if I surrendered myself to God? Would He love me and answer my prayers? He had made me, so I bet He could fix me.

It just so happened that the very next week there was a revival meeting at our church. I don't remember a single word that the minister spoke that night, but I know the stirring that was in my heart. The song "I Surrender All" was playing. The invitation was given to come forward and pray for forgiveness of sin. Satan was telling me, *No! No! No!* He used something that should have worked, but it didn't: *You will look stupid*, but this was one time I didn't care. I believed in God, and that night my life changed. I felt a peace and joy. It is so hard to explain. My countenance had changed, and my outlook on life changed. I knew that I was going to do better in school, because all things were possible.

The next day after school my mother got me aside and asked me about the night before. It was a little scary trying to explain something that I could not, because if I could, the whole world would run to the altar and pray. My mother could see the sparkle in my eye. She asked me a simple question: "Why did you go forward last night?"

As a little boy would say it, "Mother, I heard a voice in my heart tell me that I needed to."

Then she said something that I will never forget. She knelt down on her knees, looked me in the eye, and said, "Son, that voice is the voice of the Holy Spirit. Whatever you do in your life, never harden your heart to Him, and always follow Him. Do as He says, and you will be and accomplish whatever God has for you, because His plans are perfect. Never harden your heart to that voice!" Not too long after that, at another church service I was filled with the Holy Spirit and baptized with His love.

The anointing was on my life as a little boy. I remember so clearly that when I would play, when I would hunt, there was a song in my heart that flowed from deep within. I made up songs and worshiped God in spirit and in truth. That's right, *truth*. The Word of God says we must all come to Him as a child, with childlike faith.

I went back to school and worked harder than I had ever worked before. I listened to every word my teachers spoke. The struggle was the same. I could not overcome my disability. I was given a New Testament, one of those little ones that you put in your pocket. During recess I would read it. Believe it or not I could do a pretty good job. The big words I can't pronounce today but I could make sense of it. I could close it, and then try to picture the same words that I was reading and the letters would be scrambled. Totally mind boggling.

Motivated by Anger and Adrenaline

When I entered fifth grade, Mrs. Southard was gone. I had Mr. Mitchell. This guy was just the opposite. He was full of himself and lectured on and on. Previously, I always liked to listen to the teacher, but he turned me off. Condemning and preachy, he liked to make examples of people. He got joy out of putting you on the spot. Somehow he got satisfaction out of bringing me to the blackboard and making a fool out of me. Satan used that man to put hatred in my heart again.

I still carried the New Testament. I remember the day on the gym bleachers when I took it out of my pocket, looked at it, and said, "Not even God can fix me." That was the last day that I took it to school. All my high hopes had disappeared; anger filled the emptiness in my heart. Anger can feel good to that burning thing; it's a power, it can motivate.

Cheating was the only way I could survive. Mr. Mitchell knew I did it, but he couldn't prove it. I was pretty slick. One day he called me to the front of the class. He read each question from the test I'd just taken and then told me to write the answers on the board. I would turn around and just tell him the answers, which I knew, but that wasn't good enough. After I had misspelled practically every word, he laughed, along with the class. I may have hated before, but now I wanted to kill.

It just so happened the next evening after this incident we had a basketball game at Licking, Missouri. I was not a great athlete, but I was part of the team. I rode the school bus to the game. As we were unloading the bus, one of my friends said, "Look, there's old man Mitchell's truck." One look at it, and I wanted to burn it to the ground. That was a little too flamboyant, but there had to be something we could do.

It was a tournament, and we had to play two teams. It was going to be about an hour before it was time for us to play. My friend and I crawled out of the bathroom window. We didn't want anyone to see us walk out the front door of the school. It was dark, and everyone was inside watching the game. We walked up to the truck and thought, what can we do? On the end of the valve stems of the tire was a shiny bright valve stem remover. The answer came. We removed the valve stems from all four tires. Then we went back in through the bathroom window to the dressing room and played our game like nothing had happened. Of course when you do something like that you have to keep a souvenir. I put the shiny valve stem remover in my pocket.

When the game was over and the school bus was loading, we saw a big commotion around his pickup truck. The bus left. We thought we were successful. The next day at school as soon as the bell rang, the intercom instructed that everybody that had gone to the ball game last night was to report to the cafeteria. I thought, *This can't be good*, but I had forgotten all about the valve stem remover. In the cafeteria everybody was lined up along the cafeteria tables. Everybody was to empty their pockets on to the table in front of them.

I knew I was in trouble. I reached into my pocket and put the valve stem remover between two fingers. All of a sudden I had this huge urge to yawn, I flipped the remover into my mouth and swallowed it. Thank God nobody saw me and everything else went on the table. No remover was found that day, and I certainly never looked for it again. On the way back to the classroom Mr. Mitchell met me at the door. He snarled, "Goldsmith, I know you did it."

That burning anger welled up in me, and I looked him in the eye and said, "Prove it."

My sixth grade year wasn't quite as bad. I think academically some of the teachers kind of gave up on me. Also in sixth grade we started band. My parents bought me a trumpet. This was something I could do. The music teacher saw how hard I was trying and gave me praise on my progress, which was encouraging. Our school had received an invitation for our band to play at the 1964 World's Fair in New York City. What a motivator. It actually motivated the whole community with fundraisers. I still remember the songs we played. The trip to New York was something else. I will never forget the concrete jungle, Radio City Music Hall, the hotels, and the long bus ride. It was spectacular.

OCT • 63

By this time I had gotten a new horse. It was a Tennessee walking horse, and unlike my Cocoa, this horse was a little nuts. She threw me several times. She threw my sister, Lavell, in the middle of the field one day. During a horse show at Roby, the horse reared and fell over on top of me. After breaking several ribs, a trip to the hospital, and several weeks of recovery, I continued to ride. It was an anger outlet.

My mother couldn't believe I was still riding. This was a challenge I could see. Dyslexia was invisible, and I would do anything to impress my father. The love of horses, and the challenge to overcome my own fear was intoxicating. I think it is called adrenaline.

My father's health problems had gotten worse, and he had a second heart attack. The decision was made to sell the farm. Selling the farm was a shock. Dad was not able to continue farming or working and took early retirement.

Where in the world is Table Rock Lake? One trip to the area and I told myself this could be good news. Just a month or two into my seventh grade, we moved to the small community of Cape Fair, Missouri. Our new home on the lake was awesome, but it also meant a new school. Not so awesome.

The first day at Reed Springs High School all the kids were talking about the knife fight that happened the night before in front of the Nighthawk Tavern. I was interested, since this didn't happen in Plato. "Where is the Nighthawk Tavern?" I asked.

"Oh, it's right on Main Street," someone told me. "Harold Logan's mother owns it."

I met Harold right away. With me being the new kid, Harold wanted to impress me. He told me, "Ralph, we will go downtown and see the blood on the sidewalk from the knife fight." Of course, we couldn't leave school to see it, but he wanted to impress me. Also the first week of school I became involved in a fistfight.

The buses would arrive at school fifteen to thirty minutes before the bell rang. That time would be spent in the gym, where the biggest attraction was the trampoline. One morning when I was having my turn, a young man kicked me on the backside every time I landed. I warned him not to do it again, but he didn't take my warning. That boiling anger experience came out of me like a flood. I made one bounce, landed on the floor, and without hesitation began a fistfight that left him shocked and amazed. The bell rang and off to class we went.

The word was out that at lunch; he and all his friends were going to beat the crud out of me. The principal found out about it and called us both into the office, where we explained our stories. He asked, "It looks like you two have a problem. Is it over? If not, we can go into the gym where I have some boxing gloves, and we can settle it."

The young man that I had trashed responded, "It's over as far as I'm concerned." From that point on I was considered a tough guy, which felt good. If you are going to be a tough guy, you have to run with the tough guys. So Harold Logan and Jimmy Reed became the crowd that I ran with. In my heart of hearts I knew that this was not who I really was. Although I had discarded the Bible, my mother's training and the experience that I had received had not totally left me, but the peace that I had received was gone. In place of it was discontent, anger, and a sense of unworthiness, with low self-esteem. I had put on a big front, but academically nothing had changed with the determination that I would never fail a grade again.

Some of the crowd I was running with didn't have that determination. I remember studying for the test on the Missouri Constitution that you had to pass before going to the eighth grade. My teacher, Ms. Martin, allowed me to take this test several times. She called my mother and told her of my struggles. My mother and

I studied together. After failing it at least twice, I was beginning to panic.

One evening my mother received a phone call from Ms. Martin explaining to her that in the middle of the night she had received a vision of me in a position of authority, that I would become an expert on Missouri history, and that I would become successful with that knowledge. For the next week my teacher took special interest in me, tutoring me in a very kind and understanding way. Her time spent with me was appreciated. I passed the test. The very next week I was introduced to a new class that helped people with disabilities. But sadly I wanted no part of those classes. I had not recovered from the worry of looking stupid in front of people. Besides, what girl would be interested in a guy in a special class? That's right; girls were starting to get important.

Seeing Hope at a Distance

Not just any girl. During the first week at my new school I noticed a lovely young lady. She had brown hair, brown eyes, and an incredible smile. It was more than just a smile. It was radiance aglow with a presence of the Holy Spirit–filled life. I recognized that this girl lived in the realm that I once had, and it was an annoying freedom that I longed for in my heart. She was an A student and ran with all the A students. Why would she even look at me? She didn't, but I watched her.

I found out where she went to church. I found out that she went to the Galena Assembly of God church, the same denomination as my mother and I. Mother was looking for a church for us and she suggested Galena but I objected. We decided on Crane Assembly of God. I didn't want Krissy to see my hypocritical ways. You see, in front of my mother I acted like a Christian, but at school I cultivated the tough-guy image. I ran with the tough guys, but in my heart I really didn't want to be there. The other way seemed so weak, and I prayed for help, but in my mind it didn't come.

Dyslexia never left my mind, and my disability ruled every emotion. Somehow when I felt so inferior, being the tough guy seemed the only way. I saw Krissy as a representative of everything I wanted to be in my life. She was a strong Christian who shared her faith openly, showing me that she was everything that I was not.

Time went on. I had the same struggles, and Satan, as always, led me deeper and deeper, with smoking and drinking and Harold a good source for them. Since Harold's mother owned the Nighthawk Tavern, it was easy access.

I was a farm boy, in a resort area. There were two classes of students. There were the move-in kids whose parents mostly owned resorts and businesses that dealt with the tourist trade. Then you had the local students that grew up in the area. I did not fit in either group.

One of the move-in students was Galen. His parents owned the resort across the lake from our home. The resort rented cabins to fishermen along with the boat dock. Galen always had the right clothes, the right shoes, and all that was new and cool. It wouldn't change my heritage at all, with my parents being farm people. My mother made a lot of my shirts. I had no sense of style, and frankly I didn't care or even realize the importance of it. Now I realize that image is important to the way people look at you. Thank goodness I have my God, who looks at my heart.

This was before we had cars or were old enough to drive them. I would watch Galen motor his boat up the lake to Krissy's house. They went to church together and became boyfriend and girlfriend. They became the perfect couple, or so it seemed. Of course, I hated it. You see, Krissy was everything that I wasn't.

She was a good student, lived a Christian life unashamedly, and everybody seemed to love her for it. Why couldn't I have been that bold?

It's a funny thing how infatuated I was by her: if I was ever near her, literally I could not speak. Anything I tried to say came out as if I was a babbling idiot. I had no trouble taking speech in high school. It was the only class that I made an A in except shop and vocational tech. I love telling stories. Anytime I was in her presence, though, this cold clammy feeling would come all over me. I mistook it for love. I know now that it wasn't. It was God putting a mirror in front of my face.

Krissy was a cheerleader all through high school, and one year the decision was made that cheerleading practice would be on Wednesday nights. Krissy promptly informed them that if that was the case, she would have to quit. Come on now, nobody does that, but she was quite serious, and they changed the practice night. What a testimony. I thought if only I could have her in my life, I could live the way I should live. While one part of me said this would never happen, the other part said all things are possible.

Finally my senior year came. Would I have enough credits to graduate? I struggled through English classes; I took one of them twice and managed a passing grade. Then the thought of typing class was scary. How would I ever manage? I was scared stiff, but amazingly at first it wasn't too bad. I started learning the keyboard and typing the prepared pages that were handed out to us. Once I learned the keyboard with my eyes on the paper, typing wasn't as difficult as I thought. This went on for several weeks. I was proud of thirty-five words a minute.

Then one day the hammer dropped. The typing teacher, Mr. Scott, pronounced that today we were going to type by dictation. My heart dropped. Fear gripped me, and I wanted to crawl into a hole. He told everybody to put a blank piece of paper in their typewriter. He had a prepared script. He started reading at a very slow pace, which made no difference to me. I began typing the best I could, but finally he was so far ahead of me that I sat back in my chair and quit. He kept reading. He looked straight at me, but what could I do?

When he finished, he got up from his chair, looked straight at me, and said, "Goldsmith, into the hall." He walked out the door, and I followed. See, this man was also the football coach. I ran track, although I wasn't that good. A few years earlier I had quit playing basketball. When we were in the hall, he turned and looked at me and said, "You are a quitter." If he had only known how hard it is to even survive as a dyslexic person, quitting wasn't an option.

I was furious. I looked him in the eye with such intensity that he must have thought I was going to hit him. He backed up a little bit. "I'm not a quitter, but what you are asking me to do is totally impossible for me. I cannot form letters in sequence in my head, but that doesn't make me a quitter."

He looked at me with astonishment that I would get in his face like that. He said, "Oh, you are one of those." I don't know if he understood my problem, but we went back into the classroom, and he gave me a C for the class. I thank God that he didn't treat me the way Mr. Mitchell did, because if he had, I was a senior now with a whole lot of built-up anger. If he had embarrassed me in front of the whole class, I'm quite sure I would have done something violent. God was protecting me. Mr. Scott also taught business class, but this experience kept me from taking it. I regret not having a business class, but it didn't stop God from putting me in business.

We also had a vocational tech location which I was very excited about. Mr. Chamberlain taught the class. He owned a marina on the lake and had an outboard motor repair shop. I excelled in this class. Mechanical things have always come easy for me, like building a firing pin for my gun. After only a week of classes Mr. Chamberlain appointed me as a shop foreman. As shop foreman, one of my responsibilities was driving the other students from the high school to the vo-tech building. It gave me a sense of significance.

About that same time, Krissy and Galen had broken up, and this was quite the buzz. The word was that there was an argument about what college Galen was going to attend. He was a football star. I ran with him in track, and he was big and fast. Krissy was convinced that her calling in life was to be a pastor's wife. I thought maybe there was a possibility for us. I would be anything for her.

A day or so later it was time to go to the vo-tech school, but the word was out that Galen, Ben, Harold, and Sam were leaving school early. I found out that they were going to be partying that night in Branson, Missouri. *Why the mix of good guys and tough guys? Harold is part of my group!* As we were about to get into the vo-tech van, I told another friend of mine, Jim Taylor, to go ahead and drive the van because I would be skipping school with Harold. Jim became very angry, looked at me, and said, "You have been given the position of driving this van, not me. You have been in enough trouble lately; don't blow it in your senior year. Get in the van, and drive it now."

Not more than an hour or two later we were standing outside the shop of the vo-tech school. We heard sirens flying through town headed toward Branson. A cold chill came over everybody. It wasn't long until we all knew about the crash. The car had rounded a corner and hit a dump truck. Galen was killed in the crash. After looking at the car, I didn't know how anybody got out alive. After that day Jim Taylor became a very good friend.

The whole school was in mourning, and the funeral was held in the school gymnasium. I remember sitting there thinking, *How can this be? How could God let this happen?* The minister was a part of Galen's family, and he spoke about God's plan and how God uses even tragedies like this. I thought, *And I am mad at God because I can't spell.* How must his parents feel? He also said that because of this tragedy, someone in this room would be drawn closer to our Lord. A sense of conviction gripped my heart. As far as I knew, Galen went to church with Krissy every Sunday and was honest and fine. I thought about how I was living a double life, going to church on Sunday with my mother but angry at God in my heart.

A week or so later my dad asked me if I would like to have a car. I had a motorcycle and had been riding it back and forth to work in the summertime. You see, Galen had the coolest car in town, a 1965 Mustang GT. Dad said Galen's parents wanted to get rid of it. Without hesitation I said sure, but I should have given it more thought. Could you blame me? A 1965 Mustang GT—who in their right mind would turn that down? I didn't think about how Krissy had ridden in that car with him. If I owned that car, she would probably never ride in it with me. But it became my car.

The first week I drove to school, everybody looked at me like I was some dinosaur. It would never really be my car. I became even more of an outcast except to my tough guy friends. Maybe they were just too shallow to make the connection.

One night toward the end of school there was a party at Harold's house, with the tough guys and the wild girls drinking beer. Around midnight, after too many beers, we started talking about who had the fastest car. How dumb! It wasn't long before an argument led to a drag race challenge. Of course, I was right in the middle. I was too drunk to drive, let alone drag race.

Off we went like a bunch of fools to one of our favorite drag racing spots. I pulled up alongside Don Miles in his Chevy. Someone counted one-two-three, and off went Don Miles. To my embarrassment. I started off in third gear and slammed it into first gear. I would make a road race out of it and took off. By the time I even saw his taillights, I looked down and was doing eighty miles an hour.

I looked up again to see I was on a curve headed into the ditch. I remember hitting a culvert, flying into the air, landing hard in the middle of the road, spinning several times, and ending up on the other side of the road down an embankment. Harold and some other friends dragged me into their car, and off we went to hide from the police. After several hours I went back to the scene and looked at the road in front of me. I couldn't believe it. If I hadn't run off the road and crashed, I would have been dead. The road right in front of me came to a T. I would have run into a stone wall and possibly right into the middle of a house.

Why would God protect me and not Galen? From that night on I started looking for some new friends. It is amazing to me now how important your peers are to you when you're in high school.

I knew that somehow I had to get back to where I belonged. I could not follow these fools any longer.

The next week I got mad at the assistant principal and told him, "You can take this school and shove it." It almost got me expelled but my parents went to school to smooth things over. I was no longer allowed in any extracurricular activities, which was fine with me. It would help cut down on temptations. I think the school just didn't want me to go on the senior trip, and I didn't care. Incredibly, the car wasn't damaged too badly. I told my parents and the police that I had a tire go flat on me on the corner which caused the accident. I don't believe the police or anyone else believed me, but it was a good line.

Tough Guy Ended

Graduation was finally here. I remember sitting on the stage in our high school auditorium. My classmates walked out one at a time, being introduced with a list of their accomplishments, and received their awards. Setting in the back row, I once again felt that still small voice speaking to my heart. The voice in my spirit was calling me back to Him.

As they were reading the awards for the other students, I made a vow. "Lord, if You will help me and speak to my heart again, leading me to be Your follower, I know You can give better rewards than these." I was feeling like such a loser and knew that in my own power, I would never be a winner. I felt a mile away from God, but actually He was always right by my side. He draws near to the humble but opposes the proud.

The high school diploma was in my hand and what a burden was lifted. I actually felt more confident now than ever before. See, I knew how to work. Whether it was shoveling cow manure on the farm or rebuilding gasoline engines in vo-tech school, I could work with my hands. My father taught me to be responsible on the job. He became a fishing guide on Table Rock Lake. He taught me to do the same.

I worked out of the Bridgeport Resort and the Cape Fair docks. I my senior year I was being paid $35 a day. That spring Dad had even let me miss school a few days. He was sure that this was as good an education as I was getting at school. He was right. I was learning to deal with customers, convincing them that I was the best guide on the lake, and presenting myself and what I had to provide in the best light. I was a pretty good fisherman. The one line that my dad taught me was this: "Son, if you can sell, you will never go hungry." By the time school was out, I had paid my dad back for the car that he bought me and for the boat I used as a guide.

I had given my parents a lot of grief, especially Mother, while I was in high school hanging with the wrong crowd. I smoked, drank, and even got caught stealing, for which I had to go to court and pay a fine. It was quite embarrassing to my dad. I would come home late at night. Mother could smell tobacco. She was crying and praying for me half the night and I'm sure keeping my dad awake. Those prayers that my mother prayed are what kept me alive, along with my grandmother's prayers. I never really meant to be bad. I just had developed a hopelessness about having to be the stupid one. *Why can't I live up to the academic standards of my brothers and sisters?* I didn't realize that they weren't perfect either.

A week or two after graduation, Dad approached me while we were playing pool in our basement. He looked me in the eye and said, "Son, you're not living here another year. You're going to be a man and make your own way in this world. You're going to Kansas City and get a job. Your mother has cried enough tears over you. You are growing up and have to do what is right." This is the kind of man my dad was. He didn't mince words. But it was really good news to me. I wanted to get away and have a new start. My brothers and sisters in Kansas City were all involved in their church; maybe I could be too.

We called it Kansas City, but it really was Independence, Missouri. I moved in with my brother Herb. This is the one I loved dearly as a little boy, the one who gave me the .22 rifle. What an adventure. My brother was a fireman for the Independence Fire Department and built homes on the side. I remember coming up in the summer sometimes and working for him on homes that he was building. I remember watching him. I couldn't believe that anybody could work as hard as he did. He was loud and bossy but fair. He didn't ask you to do anything that he didn't do twice as hard. I thought he was the richest man in the world. His home on 27th Street was gorgeous. It had an upstairs bedroom with a bathroom, which was where I stayed. It was like having my own apartment.

Immediately we were in church every Sunday morning, Sunday night, and Wednesday night at Englewood Assembly of God. The pastor was Rev. Sharpe. He opened every Sunday morning with the same song: "It is no secret what God can do. What He has done for others, He'll do for you. With arms wide open He'll see you through. It is no secret what God can do." How encouraging! I met several young people my age, and all of a sudden I became cool. I still had my 1965 Mustang GT. No one knew the history of it. It was just awesome. These teenagers were all typical, but they all talked about Jesus.

I was invited to a CA (Christ Ambassador) rally, where an altar call was given. I went forward and prayed with some of the other teenagers. I really didn't feel the power of God that night and went mainly because they went. A week or so later on Sunday night another altar call was given at Englewood. I walked down the aisle and rededicated my life to the Lord, honestly and prayerfully, with an open heart. I prayed, "Please, God, help me live for You." For some reason I didn't have that feeling of peace that I had received when I was a little boy. I remember wondering whether it was too late for me. The experience I had when I was in the fourth grade was so profound, and I wanted that again, so I was a little disappointed. I expressed my disappointment to someone at that time. I don't remember who it was, but the explanation was that salvation was not a feeling but a step of faith, and as you walk in faith, God will bring you His peace. I thought, *I walked away from Him, and maybe it is going to take a while for Him to walk back to me.*

Everything That I Am Not

Then it happened. Our high school Sunday school class was called the Upper Room. You might say we got our name from meeting in the attic of the church. It was hot and sticky on this Sunday, hotter than usual. The lesson was on your lifelong mate, marriage, and how God intended it to be. My sister Lavell taught this class.

She started the lesson by saying "Some of you in this very room will someday be married to each other." How could she know that? But at that very moment I looked across the room, and on the left sat Misty Coleman beside a new girl. I took one look, and oh my, this was one hot girl. I literally heard a voice in me say, *This will be your wife.* My next thought was *No, she's nothing like Krissy.* She had too much eye makeup and was much too foxy. *This can't be the girl for me.* But she stirred me. Later I learned that she looked at me at the same time and told her friend, "Someday I will marry that young man," even though she had never spoken to me.

As we left the classroom and walked down the hallway, I positioned myself behind the pair. I watched her walk away. I thought, *No way; look at how she walks.* Krissy never moved like that and never would, but I did like it. Well, the chase was on. Every time I went to church, Misty and Debi were close at hand. It felt good. All through high school, not a single girl that I know of was ever really attracted to me. I didn't know it was God's plan. Sometimes Misty and Debi drove past my brother's house very slowly, hoping that they would see me. My sister-in-law told me about this. It sure felt good to know that someone cared and thought that I had worth.

Odd as it might seem, I didn't feel right about it. Krissy was still in my mind. I couldn't date Debi; it would be like two-timing. So I started making trips back to Cape Fair on the weekends and going to church at Galena Assembly of God. Anytime I got close to Krissy, that same old feeling of utter stupidity came over me. She could see that I had changed.

Truly the Lord was working in my life. I had a pretty good job working in a camper plant. They found out that I was a mechanic. My vo-tech teacher in high school was a Mercury outboard motor dealer. He found out that I was working in the camper plant and knew that the Mercury distributorship owned the camper plant. He informed them that I was his prime student and told them that I was working in the wrong place. I was promoted to their main Mercury motor distributing division. I worked in the warranty department, learning all the new technology. My boss was quite impressed with my abilities.

I was becoming more confident that the Lord was on my side. To me that meant that I might be more acceptable to Krissy as well. Going to church at Galena, I found out that Krissy was working in

Springfield at the Assembly of God headquarters. Also there was going to be a revival the next week at Galena, so I made plans to be there. The next Saturday night I was there. The revivalist was speaking on being called to the ministry. It was a moving service, and I'm not sure whether I was called to the ministry, but I knew that Krissy was called to be a minister's wife.

I went forward to pray at the end of the service. Pouring out my heart to the Lord, I said, "I'll be anything You want me to be. I just want Your presence so badly." His presence I received that night; my humble prayer He heard. Also the minister heard from God as well and called me out and told the congregation that he had received a prophecy for my life. He pronounced that I would minister and have a great ministry but that I would not work in the ministry itself and not earn a living through ministry. It didn't mean that God was not going to use me.

At that point he asked the church leaders to bring the offering plates so the church could take up an offering for me, to mark this occasion so that I would always know that God had a place for me in His kingdom and a work for me to perform. The offering was $17 and some change. At that time I didn't know how to take this. I was almost embarrassed to take the money. Nothing like this had ever happened to me before.

The presence of the Lord was very real, and I knew that God was looking out for me. My willingness to surrender all to Him had brought this about. Of course, soon Satan kept telling me that I was not good enough to be in the ministry: *God has rejected you;*

you're just a low-class person. Satan always lies to you and he is always trying to cut you down.

Not long after that I finally got up the nerve to actually ask Krissy for a date. But it was not to be. I wasn't in love with her. I was in love with an image that my grandmother had put in my mind of a perfect mate. She was a great Christian and ministered to me by her life. I tried to call Krissy the next day after she turned me down and explain this to her, but as usual I made little sense. What was it about this person that choked me up so much? Maybe in heaven I'll understand.

Back in Independence. I was in the process of rebuilding the engine in my Mustang, or should I say in the process of destroying it. For some foolish reason, I thought the faster my car went, the cooler I would be. I took a beautiful car and tried to make a hot rod out of it, but I did such a bad job that I could barely drive it on the street. It sounded great and ran great but was utterly impractical. One night, after working on my car all night long in my sister's basement garage, I looked at the stars and from the bottom of my heart I said, "Lord, if Debi is the right one for me, help her be patient with me until I get this car fixed, and then I'll take her seriously."

She waited, and now we've been married more than forty years. I know without a shadow of a doubt that she is the person that my grandmother prayed for. We couldn't be more opposite. This is good and it can be bad, but truly she is everything that I am not. Where I am weak, she is strong, and where she is weak, I am strong. This is a blessing and a curse at the same time. We can be like sandpaper to each other, but it has removed the rough edges from both of us. She has stood by my side through thick and thin and has never belittled me because of my disability. We were married July 22, 1972. What an incredible day! In my mind it was perfect.

God Was Out to Get Us

The new life began after the honeymoon. That could be a book in itself, for my wife to write. Looking back, do newlyweds ever know what they are really getting into? I don't think so. I was immature, and so was she, but God's grace is sufficient.

I knew I had to be responsible so I traded that Mustang for a 1968 Impala, a family car. I did this before we were married. By this time I had moved from the Mercury distributorship to a local marina near Lake Winnebago, Missouri. It was a pretty long drive each day from Independence. I was head mechanic, and because of my long hours and hard work, I eventually became the assistant manager.

My disability haunted me in everything that I did. Writing work orders was long and difficult, always feeling inferior. My anger about this pushed me to be more diligent in my work, to work harder and for longer hours, and to perform at a higher level than anyone else. I found myself being unethical—charging people a little more than I should by stating that my work took two hours when it only took an hour and a half, along with throwing in a few more parts than necessary.

Also my wife was being ignored when I didn't spend the proper time with her. We were so different, I was a whole lot country, and she was all city. I almost forced her to be involved in water sports. We went back to the lake on weekends with some high school friends for water skiing, camping, and doing the things I enjoyed.

We were involved in church, teaching Sunday school. I had been in church all my life and felt the responsibility of being the spiritual leader of our house. Debi was a new Christian. As young as we were (Debi was eighteen, and I was twenty-one), the church still allowed us to be Sunday school teachers, but those unethical deeds kept popping up in my life. Ignoring them grew out of the habit that I started in high school. Cheating seemed to be in my nature. After all, if God didn't want me to have to cheat, He should not have made me with dyslexia. Besides that, I was justified.

That was the unspoken message in my heart, ever since I had bought the lie a long time ago. Although I came back to the Lord and asked Him to forgive me of my sins, and I believe He did, the inner nature of my heart had not changed. Because I had struggled so long and so hard at school, it carried over into my work life. I felt it was all up to me, and I refused to fail, so in my heart I was convinced that unless I cheated a little bit, I would not have the advantage. So whenever anything came along that could give me an edge, I would jump on it. It was second nature to me.

Remember, I didn't have that holy presence that I'd received when I was young, when I rededicated my life to the Lord. I confessed with my mouth my sins, and I believe that He forgave me, but that holy presence was not constantly by my side in my daily life. At church I could feel His presence; even when teaching a Sunday school class of children, I felt His presence. But when I walked into the world in my daily life, somehow I felt it was still up to me. To perform, the burden always seemed heavy. My success in business was recognized, and my employer was always happy. I was making him money and was promoted to assistant manager. I began making more money.

One night I had a dream that I saw my friend Jim Taylor yelling out from hell asking me, "Why didn't you tell me about Jesus?" I woke up that night in a cold sweat. Remember, Jim was the one who saved my life by keeping me out of that car wreck in high school. God doesn't have to have a perfect vessel to do His work. He moved on my heart to persuade Jim to move to Independence with me, before Debi and I were married. He was a part of our wedding, and he later accepted the Lord into his heart.

I started substituting the thrill of the Holy Spirit with the thrill of an adrenaline rush. This was about 1974. I bought a 1973 Chevrolet Corvette. A fast car always brings the thrill. That wasn't enough, so I started racing boats. I had some friends, Rick Schuller and Dave Hall from Reed Springs, who had graduated a year behind me. They had recently moved to Independence near me. I witnessed to them also. I wasn't nearly as good an example as I should have been, but still, they could see that I had changed from high school. Rick would travel with me on weekends to Oklahoma, Dallas, Waco, and other places where the boat races took place. The adrenaline high that I experienced was incredible. It made me feel special. I believe to feel special is something every human strives for in life. No matter where we are in life, it drives us. Because I had not felt special earlier in life, it felt good to receive some notoriety. Overcoming the fear of a speedboat was just another horseback ride, like when I was a little boy. The challenge of pushing myself became a high as well.

Eventually there was a crash. The type of boat I raced was called a tunnel haul. These boats catch air in the front, which lifts them out of the water. In other words, you fly them, which makes them very susceptible to going airborne. That is what happened to me when I was racing in Oklahoma City. After a boat crash and a visit to the hospital, my friends brought me home late on Sunday night and carried me into the living room with a cast from my toe to my hip.

My sweet little wife was not happy. She had not been happy about any of this and had even gone to our minister for advice. She was fearful that I might even lose my life. After this incident she laid down the law: "Either the boat goes, or I go." That was not a contest because I knew beyond any doubt that this little lady was put on earth to be my helpmate. My racing career ended.

My insecurities didn't. How patient our God is. In a few short years my life had gone from a camper plant, to a warranty department for Mercury motors, to assistant manager of a marina, to owning and driving my own race boat. All this from a boy with dyslexia so bad that he could barely write a letter. I must really have been stupid to think that I was on my own. You could say I really had never charted my life in any way to this point. All the jobs, from the camper plant to the marina, were orchestrated by someone else: my brother, my high school vo-tech teacher, and my boss at the warranty department.

The next move in my life came one Sunday afternoon. Debi and I were taking a nap when the telephone rang. Debi picked up the phone to hear a familiar voice, a family friend of her father's, Mr. Everett. Everyone called him Tozy. Mr. Everett was a manager for Amoco Oil Company. He was telling my wife that there was a position open in his department. In church that Sunday morning, he had seen Debi and me in our usual location, and for some reason he felt that he should call me about the position.

Debi started explaining to me who was on the phone and what the call was about. My first thought was no, but no sooner had I thought it than this sinking feeling came over me. By now my wife was pretty sick of the boat business, with its long hours. I was pretty happy doing the mechanical work that I loved and felt this new opportunity could not be so enjoyable, but I recognized that still small voice telling me not to say no so quickly. A check in my heart came. I talked to Mr. Everett on the phone and made an appointment for an interview.

The next thing I knew, I was working for a Fortune 500 company in a four-story office building. This was a big change, but I tackled it just like everything else in my life. Mr. Everett taught me everything he knew and gave me a stack of books on boilers and A/C units that I read every lunch hour.

At about the same time the Lord moved us to a new church, Central Assembly of God in Raytown, Missouri. I believe it was the best move spiritually that we ever made. Nothing against my siblings, but when you go to church with a lot of family members you are always the baby. At Central Assembly we were looked at as individuals immediately. We were accepted and brought into the children's department, became children's church ministers, and led all the Christmas pageants. I thought to myself, *This is the ministry that was prophesied about my life.* It felt like God was truly using us.

Pastor Newby was a man with great calm and a great love for his people, and he had a unique way of presenting God's love. One of his great lines was that God is out to get you, but not in the condemning way. It was like God would move heaven and earth just to draw you near Him. I wanted to believe this in my heart of hearts. I had misconceptions about my heavenly Father, stemming from my experiences with my earthly father not believing I measured up.

About this time we had sold our first home, which we had bought from my sister when we were first married. It was a small house on Lake Drive with a little lake behind it, fitting for me. We used money that my father had saved from the sale of my horse and two cows when we sold our farm. Naturally I wanted that money during my teens to spend on cars and such, but my father would not let me have it until I was married. That was pretty smart. To me, a place to live is a place to live, but Debi believed in a little higher standard than I did. Remember, my wife was everything that I was not, thank goodness. Let's just say, she inspired me to improve our life's situation.

A house at 3808 Davidson became our next beautiful new home. It had three bedrooms and was near our favorite shopping mall and just down the street from the elementary school. By this time our first daughter, Janell, was about three years old. Debi was working at the Red Cross as a secretary. She promised she would keep this job if I would move to this new home. Two months later we found out that she was pregnant. We had more doctor bills, and who could possibly work with two little girls? If she did, all the money would go toward babysitting, so she became a stay-at-home mom to Janell and Lora.

My new job at Amoco Oil was so low-key it took some getting used to. The marine business was high pressure, with lots of overtime in the summer and boat shows in the winter. At Amoco Oil my salary was smaller, and there was no overtime. To say the least, financially things were not good. The saving grace was that Amoco Oil had a credit union, and I was able to consolidate a lot of my bills. There was no extra money.

Our tithing already wasn't that consistent, but it got much worse. Our new church seemed to love us anyway. We were dedicated to the children's ministry. I said to myself, we are doing this work for free, so maybe God will understand. Debi and I truly loved working with the children. If someone had talked to us about our unfaithfulness in giving at this time, it would have killed us.

Fortunately, God was out to get us. There was a building project going on at the church for a new sanctuary. One Sunday evening there was a motivational speaker who told stories about God blessing people who stepped out in faith. That night, many people, including several of our friends, were making faith promises for the building fund. That still small voice was speaking again: *Ralph, this is your time.* I thought, *Oh Lord, you know I'm not even paying a tithe. What can I do?* The figure of $1000 popped into my head.

I stood up and made my faith promise. It was almost as hard as going forward and giving my heart to the Lord the first time. Debi looked at me like, are you crazy? Stepping out in faith seems that way sometimes, but without faith it is impossible to please God.

Now it was the Christmas season. The Goldsmith family Christmas is always something to behold. Seven children, their spouses, and all the children and grandchildren meet every year for Christmas. It's always an overnight event. This year it was at my brother Herb's house. He was a fireman but mostly known as a custom home builder. This particular year Herb made several wooden cars and trucks out of some scraps from his shop, and they were a big hit with the kids.

I started hearing the still small voice again. One look at those cars and trucks and I heard it say that I could make those cars and trucks to sell and pay the $1000 faith promise. So I bought a few tools and borrowed some from my brother. I'm a mechanic, not a woodworker, so I had almost no woodworking tools. Away I went. Working at Amoco, I found delivery pallets lying around everywhere. I asked my boss if anybody cared if I took some home. I began cutting them apart and using the lumber from these old pallets to make wooden toys.

The late-nights began, and soon the business of Lifetime Toys and Treasures was born. My addiction to working long and hard hours had a place to go now. Amoco Oil was so laid back that it almost made me rest. It gave me too much time to think. With dyslexia I thought I was stuck doing menial work, being held back from being what I wanted to be. In my heart of hearts, almost unconsciously, I blamed God. By this time my high school friends were married and living their own lives. I was so involved in my own family that I didn't care if I made new friends. I became very isolated.

I was also very intense about fulfilling my promise to the church building program. After completing some of the toys, I took a few of them to work with me and showed my boss what I had made out of the old pallets. He was impressed but told me to keep my mind on the business of Amoco Oil Company. This man was a company man through and through: eat, breathe, and sleep Amoco Oil Company.

However, another gentleman in the company saw what I had made. Lou Harms was his name. He was an entrepreneur himself as a rock hound. He made belt buckles and jewelry from polished rocks. One day he caught me in the lunchroom. He began telling me about a company in North Kansas City, Osage Wood Crafts, that made waterbeds. He took me to the parking lot, and in his car he had some scrap wood that they had given him. This was just what I needed. It was short pieces of ponderosa pine from two–by–ten furniture grade lumber.

I went by the waterbed company the very next evening after work. When I pulled up to the back door I couldn't believe my eyes. There were piles of cut-off pieces of lumber, stacked, getting ready to be thrown in the trash. I looked for the office of the company, walked in, introduced myself, and asked to see the manager. He was a young gentleman, busy and full of spunk. The waterbed business was booming about this time. I explained to him why I needed the wood scraps that he was pitching. I offered him $100 if he would allow me to come by after work and load my pickup truck with them. He seemed astonished that I would hand him $100. I told him, one man's trash is another man's treasure. He said, "Help yourself, but just don't go into manufacturing."

That day began my story of turning straw into gold. Lifetime Toys and Treasures kicked into high gear. My relationship with Osage Wood Crafts grew deep and long as I paid him more money. I even bought big plastic bins with casters so they could move them around throughout the plant to collect their scrap wood. Then after work each night I pulled up to the back door and dumped the boards into the truck. I literally filled a third of my garage, floor to ceiling, with this lumber.

I found a pattern for a rocking horse and began my manufacturing. The rockers on the rocking horse had to be pretty long pieces of lumber, but most of the scrap was not much more than twelve inches long. There were a few longer pieces but not many, so the idea hit me to make riding horses with wooden wheels. They were an instant hit. I took some of these horses to work. The ladies at work thought they were incredible and bought them for their children and grandchildren.

I paid fifty dollars for space in one of the craft tents at the Independence Labor Day SantaCaliGon festival. It is a four-day show from 10 in the morning until 11 at night. By this time we had lots of other homemade items for sale. Debi made material for napkin and magazine holders and made lots of tole painting items. I displayed all the toys, rocking horses, back massagers, napkin holders, magazine racks and anything else I could think of to make a buck. At the end of the four days, we had made exactly $1000, and it all went to the building project.

My financial situation hadn't changed. The money that I had spent buying the wood and the new tools I had purchased had put me even further behind with my bills. My credit cards were getting out of hand. I had hoped if the business made enough to pay off the $1000 to the building project, then I could make it work for me as well. There were more and more late nights. My wife got involved with folk art pieces. I even got the girls involved.

Of course, I built a lot of stuff for my kids, rocking horses, dollhouses, baby beds for their dolls, and Barbie closets for Barbie supplies. Janell, our oldest daughter seemed to be a child who needed direction and goals to keep her on track. She made us big believers in behavior charts. We would put charts on the refrigerator, and as she would fill them in, her reward would be something that she wanted. This girl earned everything in her life, from a little red wagon to boom boxes and bicycles.

One day after school, Janell informed me that some of her peers were taking horseback riding lessons. "Please, Daddy, please,

Daddy, can I?" she begged. First of all, I didn't think that I could afford it, and second, I didn't think I had the time. We were already involved in slow-pitch softball.

I told her if she worked with me building toys I would pay her one dollar per hour. I would keep the chart for every hour, and someday she could buy her own horse. She had a glow in her eyes: *My own horse, a real horse.* "I had one when I was a little boy and you should have one too."

"Where will we keep it, Dad?"

I told her, "We will buy some land." I didn't realize it then but I was actually speaking the word of prophecy. Janell was my partner in business when we started doing fifteen to twenty shows a year.

We caught up on our bills and bought a travel trailer. I had built up five weeks of vacation with Amoco Oil. They were happy that I would use them one or two days at a time. My responsibilities there were to maintain the building, open it up in the morning, and keep the 300 ton Carrier chiller running for AC and Cleaver-Brooks boilers heating in the winter. Being off one or two days at a time seemed to meet everybody's needs.

My schedule was exhausting. Open the building at 6 a.m., work till 2:30 p.m., be home by 3:00, grab a bite to eat, and work in the basement on toy manufacturing until midnight. Get up again at five o'clock to be at work again the next day at 6 a.m. Besides that, on Sundays we were still children's ministers at Central Assembly of God. This went on for ten years.

I know it is hard to believe but I was a driven person determined to succeed. The trouble was I didn't know what success was. I still had this feeling of inferiority, that I was dyslexic and anybody who really knew me knew that I was stupid. I saw myself as a catfish—a feeder on the bottom of the lake. I was convinced that I had to work three times as hard to get the same results as somebody normal. People would ask me about all the hours that I kept, and I would tell them sleep was for customers.

Also my ethical problems hadn't gone away. My accounting practices were not always on the up and up, for instance, my true cost of sales. When you have a cheating problem deep in your heart, almost second nature, it's hard to see the truth about your own life. I told people that I was giving God the praise for my success. Deep down I resented that I had to work so hard to live at everybody else's standards. Obviously, I had not given God full control of my finances. If you have been in business you know that you can inflate your cost. God deserves and requires our first fruits, our very best. With the chip on my shoulder, I was not willing to give it. Fortunately, I serve a loving God who is patient with me. He knew that I was wounded deep within and that I didn't even realize that He loved me so much. He kept giving me opportunity after opportunity.

Speaking of opportunities, by this time, two supervisors over me had retired, Mr. Everett and Mr. Brown. After Mr. Brown had retired I was promoted to department supervisor, managing three employees. I managed the entire operation of the building, responsible for heating and cooling, plumbing, electrical, and computer room maintenance. At this time there were no personal computers. Business ran on mainframe computer room cables from the main computer room spread throughout the building to every workstation. My job was to run these cables, number each one, and move them with each employee.

What scared me was the reports that I had to file, write employee evaluations, and maintenance project proposals. God was always looking out for me. In those days we had a department called word processing. Winnie was the sweet lady who ran that department. I had made friends with her while I was just an employee, not a supervisor. The good Lord knew that I would need her as a friend. This department had devices that gave you the ability to just pick up the phone and start talking, and it would record what you said in the proper format and print it. There was no other way that I could perform my duties, and no one knew the difference except Winnie and me.

A New Goal

In my mind I was as good a Christian as anyone else. After all, we worked hard at church writing Christmas programs and working with the children. I didn't see anyone else working with the intensity that we did. I saw a church paid staff receiving praise and honor. I told myself that I didn't want that or need it. Oh, the lies we tell ourselves.

One day my wife came home and told me about this piece of property in Grain Valley, Missouri, that someone had told her about. That same day someone at my work had told me about a piece of property in Grain Valley. A coincidence? I didn't think so. We loaded up both our girls that afternoon and found the address we were told about in the Bellechasse addition. Immediately we both fell in love with the area. They were five and ten acre lots in the county, outside of Grain Valley. Janell was excited. She said, "I can have my horse now." By this time, she had racked up almost 200 hours of work.

Feeling inspired we called the real estate agent. The property was $21,000. After having several years of successful craft shows, we knew that this was attainable. We got a second mortgage on our home to purchase the land. At a family meeting that the girls were probably too young for, we challenged ourselves to pay off this land in one year. By this time I had six weeks of vacation time at work. We worked craft shows from Atlanta to Colorado. We did thirty-one shows that year. My wife, the girls, and I were focused like a laser. We thought about it day and night.

We started drawing plans for a new home with a large workshop. Until now all the manufacturing was being done in a two car garage. I thought that if I could accomplish this, I would truly be a success, and the inferior feeling would go away. My wife worked hard, my girls worked hard, but I was like a madman. It was pretty hard to live with the many arguments with my wife. She didn't like being pushed. She didn't care for all the traveling, setting up, tearing down, and living on the road every weekend. When the shows were local one of us would fulfill our commitment to church, but when we traveled away from home, the ministry suffered.

At the end of the year, the land was ours. Janell and Lora came home from school one day with a little tree. We got in our pickup and drove out to the property and planted the tree. After making the last payment to Commerce Bank, I took the family out to eat at Stevenson's restaurant for a celebration.

House plans were finalized, the house on Davidson Road was put up for sale, and excitement was high. I decided to sell the home myself so that I could save the real estate commission. It was a God thing. We had a buyer with our first showing. We split what the commission would have been so we both saved money. The problem was that the buyers wanted the house very quickly, and we hadn't even started our new home.

For most of 1988, while we were doing craft shows, we lived in our travel trailer; so I, not my wife, decided that we would live in our travel trailer while our house was being built. Four people living in a twenty-five-foot trailer. It was not an ideal situation, especially for my wife. We put all of our furniture in storage and put our trailer on a piece of property that our friends owned where they had electrical and sewer hookups. They only charged us fifty dollars per month.

What an experience! The property was located about fifty feet from a railroad track. My wife tells the story of one night when I was snoring, Lora was talking in her sleep, Janell was grinding her teeth, and trains kept going by. We had four bunk beds sitting side by side in the trailer, so there was no way to get away from me, Lora, Janell, or the train. At 2 a.m. she did get out of bed, made her way outside, and screamed with all her might. About the only time I spent in the trailer was to sleep. It was a little rougher for Debi and the girls; they had to cook, clean, and put laundry away every day. We also had a poodle living with us, which made things more interesting.

Building our new home was truly a family project. With so much help from my brother, nephew, and many dear friends, it went pretty fast. By October we were almost ready to move in. Living closer to our work by bringing our travel trailer from the railroad track to the front yard of our new home was helpful. We moved in around November 1, 1989.

While all this was going on, a bombshell had dropped at my job. Amoco Oil Company in Kansas City was going to shut down. All employees were going to be transferred to Des Moines, Iowa. Many employees took retirement. Here I was, right in the middle of the great big house project, and I learned that I would be transferred. They would buy my new home, and I would make a handsome profit. Amoco estimated that the house was worth over $200,000. I was only in debt on it $50,000. Either the IRS would tax me on the profit, or I would have to buy a $200,000 house in Des Moines.

The transfer didn't feel right to me. My whole self-worth was wrapped up in this home. I spent hours praying, "Lord, what should I do?" Uprooting my children and moving to another state was deplorable to me. Janell was convinced that a horse was just around the corner. I told the company that I would not be transferring. Uncertainty filled my heart, but through prayer, the Holy Spirit confirmed I was doing the right thing.

A new era in our lives was about to begin. At this point everything seemed to fall into place. Sure, we had good times and bad, financially and in relationships, but it was time for God to test us.

This new home that I thought would finally bring me significance in life, ended up so very empty. Striving so hard to obtain it was more exciting than actually living in it. Things of this earth never satisfy. Having just moved in, our first Christmas was the worst Christmas of our lives. We were tired, and no one felt at home in this big house. Debi was sick as a dog with a bad case of the flu. There was no Christmas spirit in our hearts, so we just went through the motions.

For a while everything seemed to be the same. Amoco Oil hadn't completely moved out of town yet. My Lifetime toy business was still going but at a slower pace. The big push was over, and a new one was about to begin. My lovely wife informed me that she and her friend were going to start college. Her lifetime desire had been to be a teacher.

I had a decision to make. Yes, this new home was beautiful but this feeling of unrest was still in my heart. I figured that it must be that this home is not paid for yet. The profits from the sale of the home on Davidson paid for a lot of our new home, so the mortgage wasn't that much—only about twice what I had made in my toy business the year before. It only made sense that in two or maybe three years I could have our home paid for. At the time I thought that paying off the mortgage made more sense than putting my wife through college. I envisioned another three years of her and the children working by my side to accomplish my new goal.

But seeing the twinkle in my wife's eyes made me pause. Our lives until this point had mostly been about me, with fast cars, race boats, and my adrenaline-rush life. Extreme work habits were all about covering up the emptiness and the lack of peace in my life. Fortunately, it was time for that still small voice to appear again. Was I going to try to crush my wife's dream or help her? She never enjoyed the craft show business. I can't tell you how many arguments we had over it. In my flesh I wanted to say, *No, work with me two more years,* but this still small voice kept saying, *Help her, help her.*

From this point on I was pretty much on my own with the toy business. Debi and her friend Becky were side by side, taking classes at the community college and traveling to CMSU at Warrensburg, Missouri. Our daughters were growing up as well and with so many school activities it was hard to get help from them. What had been an enjoyable family effort had become a_huge struggle. Manufacturing everything and traveling to the shows by myself became pretty miserable. I struggled through it.

By this time Amoco Oil had moved. I agreed to stay at the building and maintain it for the company. I was maintaining a totally empty four-story building. This gave me more time on my hands than I had ever had in my life. There was time to read, time to think, and time for that still small voice to deal with my heart. I knew that I was broken inside but I didn't recognize what was causing it. I did realize reaching my goals didn't fix the brokenness that I felt inside. So I turned my attention to my wife and our two daughters.

Janell had no more than moved into our new home until, you guessed it, she was asking, "Where is my horse?" By this time she had saved up $400 worth of credits working for me. There were no fences around our property, but it didn't matter. All I heard was *horse, horse.*

God's perfect timing intervened. I received a phone call from our good friends, Denny and Elaine. They shared that Elaine's father was dying of cancer and that he was selling all his quarter horses—racehorses. Denny explained that he was going to the track to watch them run and wanted to know if I would like to go with him. With my daughter's only thought being horses, when this phone call came it only made sense that a man who loved fast cars would have to love a fast horse. We picked up three horses, one for each of the girls and one for myself.

For the next five years I babysat a four-story office building with no one in it. I struggled through craft shows to help my wife through college. I found pure joy helping my daughters learn to ride and show their horses. Horsemanship was a perfect fit for me. I learned that showing horses in show classes was full of politics. I informed my daughters that we would concentrate our efforts on the speed events, barrel racing and pole bending. The breeding of our horses fit those events, and we became quite accomplished at them. We performed with MO-KAN Youth Rodeo and of course our 4-H group. In 1992 Janell took first place and Lora took third place in one of the most prestigious horse shows in our part of the country, the American Royal quarter horse show. It was a proud day for all of us.

Thirteen-year-old Lora Goldsmith of Grain Valley, and her horse, Dollar, receive a place ribbon from an American Royal representative at this year's Royal. Lora placed third in the pole bending competition.

Dream comes true for two area girls

Grain Valley girls win trophies at horse show

By The Examiner staff

When Ralph and Debbie Goldsmith and their children moved to Grain Valley four years ago, their knowledge of horses was, at best, limited.

But the parents dreamed of finding an activity that they and their children could pursue together. For Janell, now 16, and Lora, now 13, riding and raising horses had always been a dream.

Now, with a little advice from some friends and inspiration from the Bible, Janell and Lora have gained enough expertise in raising horses to garner first and third place trophies in a pole bending competition at the Quarterhorse Show at Kansas City's American Royal.

"We wanted to illustrate to our children that success doesn't come overnight," Ralph said. "It's been three long years of hard work and dedication to prepare our children to perform in the American Royal."

When the Goldsmiths first began training, they looked to the Bible for inspiration.

"We decided to purchase a training manual from Western Horseman and follow it like a Bible," Ralph said. "We believe that the Bible is the standard that guides and trains us in our lives so we can be productive and moral citizens. We wanted to compare training our horses to training ourselves, but we must base it on one particular philosophy."

Three days after winning at the

Janell Goldsmith, Lora's 16-year-old sister brought home a first place ribbon from the Royal. Janell and her horse, Donna, also competed in the pole bending category.

American Royal, the Goldsmith girls learned a different kind of lesson. Performing in another competition, neither girl managed to place.

"Our quest in life is always to succeed," Ralph said. "When failure comes, we must realize that lessons can be learned from that, as well. We tell our children to always let God reign in their lives and that He will help them understand all of their successes and failures."

The next great accomplishment was my wife's graduation. I was proud of her. Not only did she graduate, she graduated summa cum laude. My wife eventually received a job teaching in the Fort Osage school district, kept on attending classes, and got her master's degree. The building I was babysitting was purchased by the Kansas City school district, so all of a sudden we were both working in the educational field. My wife was happy, but I was not. Going from a Fortune 500 company to a liberal school district was quite a change. For Amoco I was in charge of everything that dealt with the building; the school district had a department for everything which cost more and was less efficient. It drove me crazy.

God's Timing Is Perfect

I had fallen in love with reading during these five years of babysitting an empty building. I read a lot of history—mainly about the Civil War—and books on horsemanship. Again, God's timing is perfect. Denny and Elaine had given me a book called *Pioneers of Jackson County*. I found it more fascinating than you can imagine. The Missouri history in this area was profound and made a great impression on me. I couldn't believe I had lived all my life in the great state of Missouri and was clueless as to what really happened, especially in Jackson County. Independence, Missouri, is truly where it all began.

My sister-in-law Marsha Armstrong had opened a new business on Independence Square called Bess's Tea Room, named after Bess Truman. The suggestion was made that I might start a carriage operation with my horses on the square. I had thought of that idea years earlier and had dismissed it. For the first time, I was miserable on my job. All my past jobs had been arranged for me by either my brother, my vo-tech teacher from school, promotions on jobs, Mr. Everett with the Amoco Oil position, and now the Kansas City school district. I had literally been moved from place to place almost without thinking about it. The carriage business seemed very different. I first agreed to do it part-time if a license could be acquired. It took several months, and once that took place, I became very uneasy. All visible signs on Independence Square were not what you would call booming. Yes, the history was there, but even I knew that it would be difficult.

I was uneasy. I had never made a decision like this before. I talked to the school principal where I was worked and told her what I was contemplating. This lady was a hard-working principal. She loved the children very, very much. I liked her but felt badly that she was working in a flawed system. She told me that schools would definitely be interested in the idea of doing school field trips in a covered wagon on the historic Independence Square.

That still small voice was speaking, but I was scared to death. Deep in my heart I wanted to go for it, but my flesh said, *Are you crazy? Small businesses rarely make it.* This is one time that I truly stepped out in faith. During this time of decision, I was taking steps forward, building covered wagons and carriages. I had one horse capable of pulling a carriage, but the others were crazy racehorses. I knew that only God could have prepared me for this. The five years of reading horsemanship books and history had to be His hand, and of course, my misery at my job. I had been working at the same salary for almost ten years. My wife was now making a fair income, which helped, but money was still tight.

At last the time of decision had come. I laid a fleece before the Lord. If my brother would loan me the money to buy a new team of Belgian horses. I would go full-time—and he did. What a brother. I wanted to keep my overhead as low as possible. I already had a truck, horse trailer, and covered wagons. The adrenaline was high, but reality soon sank in. Being self-employed, totally self-employed, was completely new to me.

I tackled this just like I did everything else in my life. I worked at it like a crazy man from six o'clock in the morning until 10 o'clock at night. I would bring one horse for daytime work and another for night work. More hours means more income, right? Some of the store owners made comments like "Do you ever go home?" Feeling pretty overwhelmed. I received a lot of what I call sympathy rides. People would ride because they felt sorry for me, knowing I would fail.

One couple, Jerry and Cindy Neer, rode with me often. They were my encouragers. They gave me books to read and inspiring stories of characters on the square. One was on Harry S. Truman, along with many others. I read the book on Truman, the David McCullough book, and gained a new perspective. The more I learned, the more enthused I became. Knowledge is an incredible thing; however, enthusiasm didn't help the finances. My total gross receipts for my first year were $12,868. It didn't take a rocket scientist to figure out that I might be in trouble.

My wife, God bless her soul, for the first time in our lives was making more than triple my gross receipts. She was paying all of our household bills. I remember wondering how long our marriage would last, but God knew from the beginning of time the perfect lady that He had planned for me. My grandmother prophesied it for me when I was in the fourth grade.

My second year rolled around. Early that spring I was in my carriage near the farmers' market, hoping to pick up some riders, when a young man approached and asked me to take him to his lady's apartment. I asked where it was, and he said Hocker Heights. This was down Truman Road on the other side of Nolan Road. The temperature was in the high 80s, a very warm spring day. Everything within me wanted to tell him no. I figured he had no money, but what was I here for? That still small voice spoke within me and said, *Take this man where he wants to go.* I don't know if it was my faithfulness to follow the Holy Spirit or if I was just bored but I said, "Get in," and off we went.

It was probably three quarters of a mile or more. I let him off at the apartment, but he asked me to wait, and he went to the door. A lady came to the door, and they stood there for a few minutes while I assumed he was explaining himself to her. When he was finished, she broke down in tears and hugged his neck. Then they both came back to the carriage and asked me if I would take them to her parents' home. Again I wanted to say no but could not. After asking where that was, I started off on another ride as long or longer to her parents' home on the other side of William Chrisman High School. They got out of the carriage and went to the front door. After a few minutes the same scene repeated. More hugs and tears.

By this time I had figured that something was going on, although I wouldn't be nosy. My flesh said, *Get this over with and get back to the square*, but God wasn't done. On the way I turned a corner down back roads, and all of a sudden from my left I saw a snow-white dove. I know the difference between a dove and a pigeon, and this was a snow-white dove. It fluttered right in front of us and landed on a post beside the road. I stopped the carriage and explained to my passengers the significance of a snow-white dove. It's a sign of the Holy Spirit, and believe me my spirit was dealing with me. I turned around, and they both had tears in their eyes. I took them back to their apartment. As they were getting out of the carriage, the young man handed me twelve dollars. *Well, I'm back to making what I used to make in high school, six dollars an hour.*

By the time I got back to my trailer, my horse was soaking with sweat. The Spirit was gone. I was back to feeling depressed, after spending half my day for twelve dollars. While I was washing off the horse, this sense of condemnation hit me. The voice seemed different this time. I started arguing with the Lord: *Why did You allow me to be in this position? I am failing. Can't You see?* The Spirit spoke more clearly than I had ever experienced in my life. An overwhelming feeling gripped me with a closeness that I can't explain.

He revealed to me the reason I was in this position. *I am only answering the prayer you prayed when you were a little boy on your horse Cocoa, when you asked Me to show your mother that you could be a Christian cowboy.* I had totally forgotten about that prayer. He also revealed to me that I was to operate my business in a different way. All those hours that I was putting in were not needed for my success. I was to trust Him, not myself, and to give rides free if I needed to. Success would come, but in His timing.

The Lord wasn't done with me that day. Later on I was giving a tour to a retired couple when they asked me how I got into this business, opening the door for me to witness to them. Shortly after I explained the love of the Lord to them, a car barreled recklessly around the corner and barely stopped before hitting us. That very instant the still small voice said, *I can protect you, as well.*

I went home early that night, and guess who was there waiting for me. Yes, it was my mother. I told her everything that had happened that day. I told her of the prayer that I had prayed as a little boy and how God had revealed to me today that from this day on, I must trust Him.

I know beyond any doubt that I'm doing exactly what God has called me to do. I meet people from all over the world and I'm always looking for a way to testify to them God's love and mercy. *Trust* is a word that we use, but do we really put it into use in our lives? If you had asked me before this point if I trusted in the Lord, I would have said of course I did. The truth was that I hadn't fully trusted the Lord since I was a boy in the fourth grade. That was why I had the inner unrest in my life.

Yes, I believed that Christ died on the cross and that my sins were forgiven, but because of my disability and the trials of my life, I believed my success, or what I thought was success, depended on me. My dyslexia He didn't take away, so I felt abandoned by God, who claimed all things are possible by His power. I was doomed to be the catfish, the bottom feeder, which meant that I would have the low class jobs, and to succeed meant crazy work hours. I remember going to work the next week, sitting in my carriage, and thinking, *Lord, if I trust You, then something has to change.* For the first time I knew the change needed to be in me. I also realized that this business was not mine. God had planned it from the beginning of time. If He planned it, success was His responsibility, not mine.

I cannot tell you the sense of peace that brought to my heart. I always had a peace about where I would go if I died but very little peace about my daily life. I always felt that the odds were against me. I had to learn that if God brings you to it, He will bring you through it!

The Show-Me State

Shortly after this experience, our good friends Denny and Elaine came to our home for an evening of playing cards and visiting. That night while they were there, they explained a new video series called The Truth Project. Elaine's brother-in-law had developed the series, and they would be one of the first Truth Project home groups. It was going to be a twelve- to thirteen-week series one night a week, and they wanted us to be a part of it.

At the time I thought that was quite a commitment. They explained to us that for weeks before the meetings started, they would be praying for each person who attended. After the first week I knew that this was something special. From the first night to the last my heart was stirred. I knew I had lived a life of lies, although I didn't know how deep they were. The human heart is so wicked that no one can know it. Satan had filled my life with assumptions that were lies.

After completing the Truth Project I questioned almost everything about where I stood before the Lord and the truth about my life. I prayed the notorious prayer, *Lord, please show me the truth about my life.* This is the "show-me" state you know, and for the next seven nights, while I lay in bed, the Lord revealed my life to me.

It was like a movie, with no sleep, for seven nights. Much of it I cannot put in this book, but it is the reason for this book. I want to show the love and mercy of my Lord, not the wickedness of my own heart. Self-righteousness is not righteousness. So much of my life I justified because of that catfish mentality. We are all sinners saved by the grace of God. We are not saved just to be saved, but to live in Him and through Him.

Once I faced the reality of my life with confidence that all things are in His hands, all fear was gone. I didn't realize it, but my reason for working all those crazy hours and doing those dishonest acts was that I didn't truly trust in the Lord with my daily life. Knowing that He is in total control, casting out all fear, I no longer ask God to bless me. My prayer is *Please, Lord, let me be a part of what You want to bless. May my life be a blessing to all I come in contact with, and may Your Spirit guide my every word.* If the blessings of God are not in our own hearts, then how can we pour out blessings to others? We cannot draw from an empty well.

Dyslexia was my excuse and I blamed God for it. After wrestling with an angel for seven nights—which I call it my Jacob experience—I realized that it was a blessing. Paul prayed that God would remove his thorn in the flesh, but God said, "My grace is sufficient." Ephesians 2:10 says, "For we are God's workmanship, created in Christ Jesus to do good works, which God prepared in advance for us to do."

Dyslexia forced me to concentrate on the natural talents that God had given me. As a little boy I was always trying to please my earthly father. I wanted his respect so badly that it caused me to step out where a little boy usually wouldn't. For example, I took a scrap bolt and pounded it flat to just the right thickness and filed it down in just the right shape to make a new firing pin for my .22 rifle. It still works today in that same rifle. Soon I'm going to show my grandson how to do the same thing. How about building a two-wheeled card out of some planter wheels and two small trees cut down with a hatchet and attached to the axle? Of course, my dad told me I would get killed in it, but the process had begun.

Slowly He gave me the confidence to tackle almost any project. I was bold enough to show my fourth-grade teacher the proper way to use a handsaw. Playing the trumpet became a point of confidence, and I even won awards in competitions and at state band. The list goes on. Anything that had to do with writing or spelling gripped my heart with fear. The total embarrassment of misplacing letters or turning them around and the giggles in the background would literally make me sick to my stomach. But the inspiration of building something was a lift to my heart.

My vo-tech classes came with the same result when my teacher recognized my confidence with mechanical things and made me shop foreman. Which most likely saved my life, because I was in charge of driving the van to the vo-tech school when Jim Taylor insisted that I drive it, on the day Galen was killed in the car accident. Being made fun of a lot made me very aware of facial expressions and body language. I seem to have a sixth sense of when people are having a good or bad experience, whether they are receiving what I'm saying or tuning me out. The only class in high school that I made an A in, other than shop and vo-tech, was speech and especially storytelling. My teacher was an incredible lady. It was the first time I was given the stage with a sense of power, and the audience couldn't talk over me. When I was given full control, storytelling became intoxicating.

I wanted to be in the school play so desperately, it was all that I could think about for weeks. But the readings for the different parts scared me to death. Stumbling on the words or being completely unable to pronounce a word would mean a bad score. I begged my speech teacher to allow me to read the parts ahead of time, but she refused. I could not explain to her why I wanted to do this, because it would be admitting that I had a problem. Or in my father's words, *You're not stupid, so don't act like it.* I was consumed by hiding my dyslexia; the embarrassment of being considered stupid was intolerable.

But the tough guy crowd accepted me with open arms. They were just as messed up as I was but in a different way. To be with this crowd meant smoking, drinking, cursing, and showing hatred for the goodie-good crowd. In my heart of hearts I didn't hate them; I hated the snickering and nonacceptance. Krissy seemed different with her glowing spirit and her smile. I knew where it came from once I had it.

But soon school was over. I seemed to excel in all things that meant working with my hands: marine mechanic, boiler operator, electrician, toy manufacturer, home builder with my brother, carriage and covered wagon manufacturer, horse and mule trainer, and my latest, furniture maker. These were the gifts that God gave me.

I realize now there are no low gifts or high ones. There is no catfish mentality; we are all top feeders or largemouth bass in God's eyes. For we are God's masterpieces. C. S. Lewis said your real, new self will not come as long as you are looking for it. It will come when you are looking for Him. The biggest lie of all is that you can have your true identity outside of God. This is a lie that Adam and Eve bought.

I was running from God, and all the time He was pushing me towards the gifts that he had designed for me all along. What a loving God. Psalm 139:16 says that "your eyes saw my unformed body. All the days ordained for me were written in your book before one of them came to be." What joy and peace if that is truly deep within your heart of hearts. Every day of my life was recorded, every moment laid out. Jeremiah 29:11 says, "'For I know the plans I have for you,' declares the Lord, 'plans to prosper you and not to harm you, plans to give you hope and a future.'" Let me add, the suffering that we think we are going through only moves us toward His perfect plan. His plan is always to move us closer to Him. I believe God asks for trust before He gives revelation.

Ministry Title

One of my favorite movies is *Forrest Gump*. Forrest is a person with challenges of all kinds, physical and mental. His mother has explained to him that life is "like a box of chocolates: you never know what you're gonna get." In everything that Forrest does, he comes out on top by the end of the movie. I think even he realizes life is not a box of chocolates, for there is someone with a plan.

Another movie I love is *It's a Wonderful Life*, because this one represents my philosophy of life. I thought that I wanted to be a minister, and I am. Ministry is our life and how we live it. Every word we say and every person we meet affects the future. We will stand accountable for every word we speak and every action. It is very exciting to know that every single one of us can be a part of God's kingdom. Not having a ministry title doesn't mean we don't have a ministry. We are the church. Church services are held every day, in every word we speak and with every smile.

Living life for your own benefit is empty and without reward. You cannot outgive God. The more you give the more you receive. It is not all monetary. Believe me, I have been blessed. When I started Pioneer Trails Adventures, I vowed that I would give at least 10 percent of my gross receipts. No playing around with the books;

firstfruits means "first fruits" (see Proverbs 3:9). Now not only do I have a business that I love, but it is growing and prosperous. I have more materially than I ever believed I would have.

But that is not the success that I treasure the most. Real success is having the same joy and peace that I experienced when I was in the fourth grade. Having His Spirit flow from me means more than anything in the world. If you go through The Truth Project, the number three will become very special to you: mind, body, and spirit; Father, Son, and Holy Spirit; husband, wife, and children; executive, legislature, and judiciary. The Bible says a three-strand rope is very hard to break. The examples of three can go on and on. Now I wish I had three children instead of two.

God has intervened in my life countless times. He has protected me from motorcycle accidents, car crashes, and boat racing accidents, too many times to mention. Why would God spare me when sometimes He doesn't spare others? Maybe because He wanted me to write this story of my life, which the still small voice has been urging me to do for years. My fear of writing stopped me, but thanks to computer technology I am now able. Maybe it is God's timing again; be anxious for nothing.

The God I serve brings everything about at the exact right time. If we do things in the flesh, even good things, the timing is never right. Have you ever tried to witness to someone without the Holy Spirit leading you? It never works, because if the Spirit is not calling, no one can come to the Lord. "Not by power, nor by might, but by my spirit, saith the Lord of hosts" (Zechariah 4:6,

KJV). According to George Washington, we cannot build a nation without the hand of God; neither can we build our lives without His hands guiding us each day.

Every single person on this earth has one disability or another. God chooses not the high and mighty but the humble. Your disability may not be the same as mine, but you are a masterpiece. You may have an IQ of 140 or 50, but God has a plan. A superior mind may give self-confidence, but confidence in the Lord is much better. Lean not on your own understanding, but commit all your ways to the Lord (see Proverbs 3:5; Psalm 37:5). That is not to say we should not make plans for the future. Proverbs 3:6 says we should lay our plans before the Lord, and He will guide our path.

Would I really want to go somewhere or do anything without Him? I don't think so. Proverbs 1:33 says, "Whoever listens to me will live in safety and be at ease, without fear of harm." When my mother told me about that still small voice, when I was just saved, it was the best advice that I ever received in my entire life: "Son, never harden your heart to the voice. It will always lead you to good things." And it has.

But there is one other voice, and this one is loud. This voice tells me how stupid it is to write these words in the first place. Sadly, this voice sometimes carries the day; during too much of my life, it did just that. We all know where it comes from, always spreading the lies. It gets a hold in your life, through fear, greed, hatred, lust, the poor-me mentality, or the catfish mentality. Thank God for His love and mercy to rescue us from the snare.

Yes, I am back to where I was when I was in the fourth grade, believing that all things are possible, in God's timing. You see, to be right with the Lord, you must come to Him as a child, whether you are nine or ninety-nine years old. I am excited about the rest of my life. Each day is a new adventure in God, not in me, because all power flows through Him. And when this life is over, my greatest passion will be to tell my story during the thousand years of peace when Christ Himself rules on this earth. For I will be one of His servants to tell the multitudes about how God preserved a dyslexic little boy who thought he was a bottom feeder—who thought it was all up to him to be successful, trying to gain the respect of his earthly father, but learned that his heavenly Father loved and respected him all through the process.

That loud voice in my head tells me to keep going, talking about all the blessings of God and where I've been and what I've been through, but the still small voice is telling me to shut this thing down. God's message to us is a simple one; even a child can understand. We have a wicked heart, and everyone is without excuse. The stars above, the earth below, and everything that crawls or walks has a master. Chickens have a pecking order; horses and mules have the dominant female and male in the herd. Solomon said, watch the ants, they work in perfect order with the queen ant.

We have no excuse; we are God's children, created by Him, for Him, and for His good pleasure. When I train mules and horses, at first they do not wish to come under my control. But when the training process is done, not only do they become productive, but their gentleness allows me to care for them in a gentle way. Therefore, they are healthier and live longer. Whether it is you or a stubborn mule, I believe happiness comes by being productive.

God created the universe and all that we see. We are created in His image. That means that we are creative beings ourselves. Just look at the world, from the New York skyscrapers to space shuttles to craft taking two men to walk on the moon. How can anyone say that we are not creators ourselves created in the image of the great Creator?

One more piece of advice from my mother. She was always saying, "Waste not, want not." God takes people who are discarded by others and uses them for great things. All through my life I've always done my best to have as little waste as possible in my life. That is with material things as well as my time. Time can never be recovered.

When God's still voice speaks to you, act. Learn to hear His voice, and step out in faith. God's voice will never lead you wrong. Remember, timing is everything. Whenever He speaks to your heart is the time to act. Do not rationalize; do not depend on your own understanding. Make sure your motives are pure, and step out of the boat. You can walk on water just as Peter did, and as long as you keep your eyes on God and your mind off this world, you will stay afloat.

The first time in my life that I ever really stepped out of the boat was when I quit my job with the Kansas City School District and started Pioneer Trails Adventures. When anybody starts a new business they are full of hope and expectations. I believed in that still small voice and knew it was God's calling. After one year in business I started looking at the wind and the waves of the $12,000 gross receipts of that year. Just as Jesus reached out and took Peter by the hand and pulled him to safety, so my Lord did the same for me.

His hand was sending me to the young man that I took to Hocker Heights to meet his lady. At the time I didn't realize that it was God's hand. With my willingness to follow the still small voice, He showed me His glory. From then on, God has been revealing Himself to me more and more deeply each day. What a relationship that I have with my Lord. Therefore, my relationships with my wife and daughters have improved. Also he has sent me help in my business, with people who could work for me at a rate that I can afford. He has given me the opportunity to bless them, even before they bless me. Give and it shall be given unto you.

Who knows what the future may bring, and the past is no guarantee of the future. I know who holds my hand. When God is for us, then who can stand against us? All things work together for good for those who are called according to His purpose. I ask You, Lord, always keep me on the path of Your purpose. I may never speak from great pulpits or fill auditoriums. My wagon seat is my pulpit, and if there is only one person in my wagon for my life to influence, then so be it.

No two people have the same calling. If your calling is to surf with one arm, after a shark has bitten the other off, then surf and be a witness. If your calling is to work in a dead-end job, then stay there. If the still small voice calls you out of the boat then do not be afraid. David killed a giant with one stone because he knew God, and he walked with Him daily.

Once we hear the gospel and accept Christ as our Savior, the Holy Spirit seals us and guarantees a life in Christ. That promise comes true, not through us but through the power of the Lord God Almighty. He seals us and protects us and holds us in His heart. As long as we keep Him in our heart, even if it is a tiny crack in our heart, God has guaranteed our inheritance.

Many people accept Christ and grow disappointed in their walk. They feel that God has not lived up to their expectations. They walk away from the church. Are those people lost forever? Have they rejected God totally and completely? In my case, no. I think in many cases they have gotten hurt and walked away, but the grace of God covers their life. If I had gotten in the car with Galen and been killed, I believe that God would have taken me to heaven, because His grace carries me. In my heart I wanted to serve Him, but I didn't know how. I felt that I'd been gypped and that I was a victim, and I could not serve Him because of it.

My most sincere prayer is that you never harden your heart to God's voice.

The still small voice can be very difficult to distinguish from your own. Listen carefully.

As Peter called out to the Lord, "Is it You?" and "If it is You, bid me to come." (See Matthew 14:22–32.)

Each time we step out in faith, God is faithful and just to confirm it in your heart.

And each time that He does confirm His voice, it is clearer and more distinct.

I dedicate this book to everybody with disabilities and that is all of us: we are all flawed, sinners prone to follow our own passions. God's trail is narrow, and few find it, which breaks my heart. The riches at the end of this trail are so much greater than all the gold in California that American pioneers traveled for months to find, crossing our nation for earthly treasures. The treasures of our Lord are free. The only price is our surrendered heart and life. They are free for all who believe in our Lord Jesus Christ.

As my boyhood hero would always say, "Happy trails, and may the Lord take a liking to you." Happy trails to you until we meet again, whether here on earth or in heaven.

CPSIA information can be obtained
at www.ICGtesting.com
Printed in the USA
BVHW032034190222
629514BV00001B/2